WALKING

—THE—

LINE

Discoveries Along the
Los Angeles City Limits

Roy A. Meals, MD

Published by Boundary Line Books.

Library of Congress Control Number: 2025915295

ISBN 979-8-9995777-0-2 (paperback)
ISBN 979-8-9995777-1-9 (ebook)
ISBN 979-8-9995777-2-6 (audiobook)

PRAISE FOR *WALKING THE LINE*

"Walking the Line links seemingly disparate topics such as peacock crossings, cemeteries of the rich and famous, perils of climbing sandstone, and bee keeping. In the process, Meals touches your heart, mind, and funny bone."

SPIKE CARLSEN, author of *A Walk Around the Block*

"Roy Meals has explored the city at length, obviously, but also at great depth. This story of the plots, personalities, and peccadilloes that shaped Los Angeles is fascinating."

CHARLES FLEMING, author *Secret Stairs: A Walking Guide to the Historic Staircases of Los Angeles*

"What a story he tells of life at the edge of America, the City of Angels, where dreams are made."

SHANE O'MARA, author of *In Praise of Walking: A New Scientific Exploration*

"Hardly anyone knows the geography of LA's crazy outline like Roy Meals, who has walked its jagged miles. Take this journey with him and see the city as never before."

D. J. WALDIE, author of *Elements of Los Angeles*

"An inspirational account of walking the borders of Los Angeles, combining history, science, geography and so much more. Roy reminds us that the only way to truly understand and know a city is by walking it."

ANNABEL ABBS-STREETS, author of *52 Ways to Walk: The Surprising Science of Walking for Wellness and Joy, One Week at a Time*

Also by Roy A. Meals, MD

The Hand Owner's Manual
Bones, Inside and Out
Muscle, The Gripping Story of Strength and Movement
Ligaments, Appreciating the Bands That Bind Us

CONTENTS

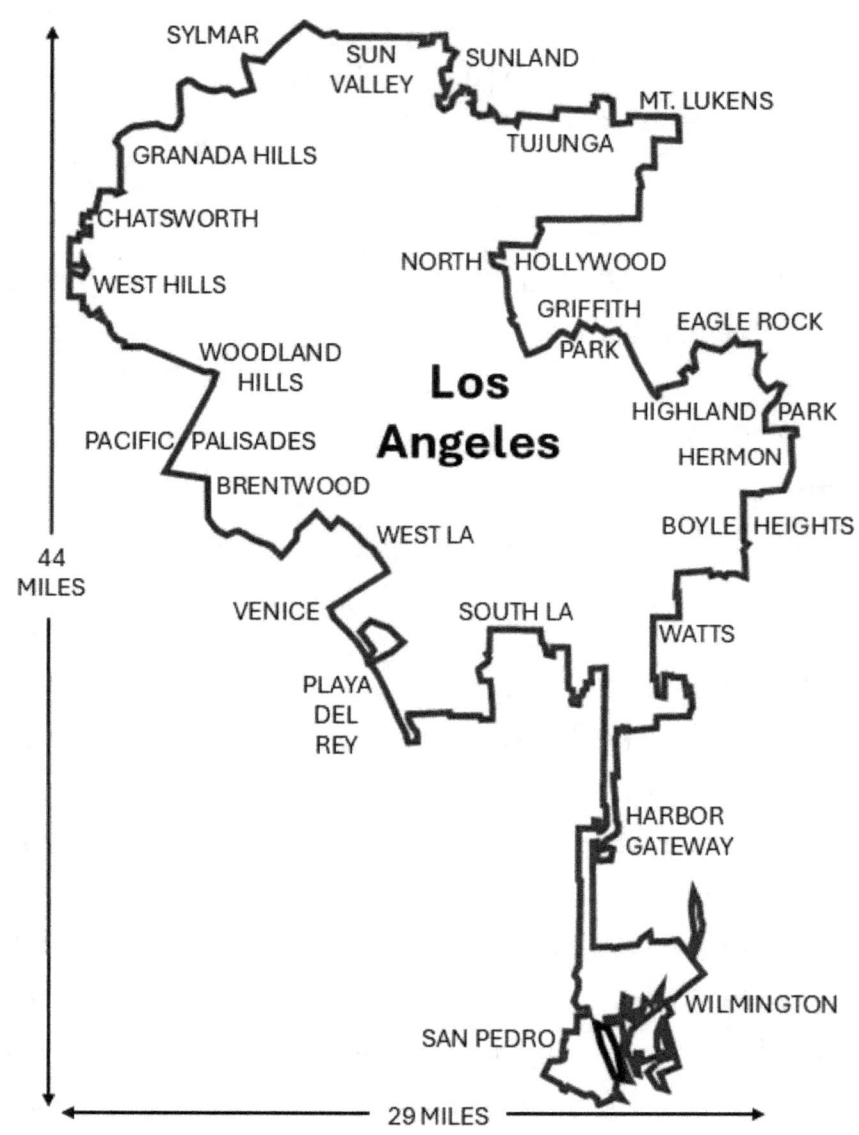

CHAPTER 1

HEADING OUT

An imaginary line on the earth's surface, 342 miles long, zigs and zags at irregular intervals and finally doubles back on itself to end where it began. So arranged, it encloses 467 square miles of land and 34 square miles of water. The land is almost half the size of Rhode Island.

Despite the apparently insane, erratic course of this unseen line, each angle is legally documented within a small fraction of a degree, and the length of each segment is precisely recorded to less than an eighth of an inch. It defines the city limits of Los Angeles, home to nearly four million residents. (For clarity, the vastly larger Los Angeles County engulfs the City of Los Angeles and 87 smaller ones plus some unincorporated areas. It is over three times the size of Rhode Island and shares with it a somewhat rational-appearing outline. For brevity, whenever I write *Los Angeles* or *LA*, I am referring to the city by that name.)

In the beginning, Los Angeles City was also sensibly shaped, a square that measured about two miles on each edge, but that was back in 1781. Maybe the world was rational then, but myriad pressures in the interim forced changes. What started as a Native American village became a Spanish outpost that slowly morphed into the second-largest city in the United States, famous for the thrill and glamour associated with its thriving entertainment industry. Iconic attractions include the Hollywood Bowl, Hollywood Walk of Fame, Hollywood sign, La Brea Tar Pits, Sunset Boulevard, Dodger Stadium, Griffith Observatory,

SoFi Stadium, Universal Studios, Getty Center, and Disney Concert Hall. These world-class attractions tend to clump toward the middle of this strangely shaped city.

Centralization offers efficiencies for business, transit, and sight-seeing but means that interesting attractions on the periphery may be overlooked and underappreciated. And even though the city is famous for its infatuation with cars, both for transportation and self-esteem, Angelenos tend to travel mostly within their own neighborhoods. Residents in Santa Monica and Brentwood express few reasons to ever venture east of the 405 Freeway, and those in Beverly Hills tend not to go west of it. The same can be said for Pasadena versus the West Side and the San Fernando Valley versus The Basin.

Two forces are likely to be at play: familiarity and traffic congestion. I hear, "Why get stuck in traffic in an unfamiliar area? I'd rather stay close to home." These factors are amplified by a sense of security associated with staying in one's own car and in one's own neighborhood. I counter, "How boring. You live in one of the greatest, most culturally and ethnically diverse cities in the world, yet you don't explore it or take advantage of the experiences it offers." For these reasons, I decided to explore the margins of Los Angeles City on foot—an adventure aimed at keeping me mentally and physically agile.

My interest in adventure goes back at least to junior high school. I remember savoring World War II prisoner-of-war escape books and later reading the near-death accounts of Shackleton's and Amundsen's polar explorations and Teddy Roosevelt's foray into the South American jungle. Even though I would have liked to be at Amundsen's side when he reached the South Pole, I don't consider myself a daredevil. I have no desire to bungee jump, skydive, or climb glaciated mountains, but I do thrive on strenuous outdoor activity; and I take more risks, which I consider controlled, than some people. Past adventures include taking the "polar plunge" off the coast of Antarctica, summiting Kilimanjaro (elevation 19,341 feet) at sunrise, hiking the Grand Canyon rim-to-rim twice, riding my bike 250 miles down Pacific Coast Highway from

Monterey to Santa Barbara, and walking narrow trails with precipitous drop-offs on the way up Mount Whitney (elevation 14,505 feet)—the highest peak in the lower 48 states.

Running the Los Angeles Marathon at age 61 was also adventurous. My foremost discovery was that I was not designed to run 26 miles. It took three consecutive marathons before that insight sunk in. During these runs, however, the tour through previously unexplored ethnic neighborhoods that I shared with 22,000 other runners was eye-opening. The experience "connected" me with Los Angeles, my fellow masochists, and enthusiastic spectators lining the course. The festive event cast a spell over me and gave me a heightened sense of ownership and pride in our city.

In integrating these experiences with a strong feeling of wanting to stay active, I hatched a plan to explore the boundaries of Los Angeles. It would be a daytime adventure. I'd sleep at home every night. It would get me out of the car and out of my neighborhood and invite discovery. It might tempt other Angelenos to do the same. More broadly, it might inspire curious people everywhere to explore their locale more widely and maybe even do so on foot.

The precedence for walking adventures goes way back. Consider Marco Polo's trek to China and the pilgrims' journey to Canterbury, whose stories Chaucer recorded. In modern times, devout Christians tread the Camino de Santiago in Spain, and walkers of all types hike the 2100 miles on the Appalachian Trail from Georgia to Maine and 2600 miles on the Pacific Crest Trail from Mexico to Canada. Also several runners and walkers have created unique adventures for themselves. Jack Witzig has run every street in Camden County, New Jersey, over 2200 miles. Following Jack's lead, Michael Lisicky jogged every street in his hometown of Baltimore, 5 to 8 miles a day over 8 months. Angelenos Tucker O'Neill and Wes Braumbaugh walked 40 miles across our city in 14 hours. All of these remarkable feats, running, walking, limping, were, however, more about the destination than the journey. The primary goal for each was to finish.

Two Angelenos have made long treks across the city that did stress journey over destination. A mother-daughter duo photographically documented Wilshire Boulevard over its 15-mile course from downtown to the ocean, and a food writer gastronomically toured Pico Boulevard's similar length, sampling the fare at every eatery en route. So too, my trek focused on the journey. Destination was not the issue because I would finish where I started.

Planning my trek was agonizing. I started with an accordion-folded paper map of Metropolitan Los Angeles published in 1978, one that the American Automobile Association and filling stations used to hand out in pre-computer times. You may remember when AAA maps and the Thomas Guide were the only navigation aids available. (By the way, Thomas Guides are still available and are of particular use to first responders out of cell phone range. I recently bought the 56th Edition, 2022, but its detailed maps were too compact and disjointed from page to page to serve my pedestrian purposes.) The AAA map helped me with general orientation and to differentiate areas that had been previously confusing to me—such as Bell Gardens, Garden Grove, Hawaiian Gardens, and Gardena.

After getting generally oriented from the paper map, I went electronic and scrutinized Los Angeles on navigatela.lacity.org. This website displays a fine-grained map of the entire county of Los Angeles. When maximally expanded on the computer screen, navigatela shows every parcel of real estate and a footprint of the structure(s) on it along with the street address. An overlay line clearly indicates city boundary lines, which sometimes, strikingly, cut through the middle of individual plots. This resource does not, however, include names of any potentially interesting stops. For those, I turned to Google Maps, which, when expanded, identifies many such locations. From the screen, I copied the address of each site that looked interesting and pasted it into nagivatela's search bar. That pinpointed its location, and a nifty measuring tool embedded in the website measured the distance of that location from the Los Angeles City limits. To make my trek manageable, attractions of potential interest had to be within a mile inside the city limits. Individually owned eateries, bookstores, and animal rescue missions attracted my attention. Home Depot, Burger King, and other multi-location, homogenized enterprises did not. Attractions that were outside of the city line would have to wait for a future adventure.

By this means I identified over 200 potential stops that were less than a mile inside the 342-mile perimeter of Los Angeles City. To these, I added attractions from such lists as *Best Food Trucks in LA* and the *Historical Marker Database*. The next equally tedious step was arranging these stops in a somewhat linear order to minimize backtracking. This was complicated when a freeway cut across a potentially walkable route, which necessitated taking a circuitous course. More often I also had to backtrack to a site on a different day or time to match opening hours. Some points of interest were only open on Sundays, others on all days except Sunday, some once a month, others by appointment. Another necessary compromise was that I could not walk precisely on the city-limits line since, rather than running down the middle of a street, it often took crazy turns through residential backyards and commercial freight depots and across golf courses and cemeteries. So I stayed as closely inside as I could.

From training walks, I knew that I could comfortably walk ten miles in less than three hours; but for the trek, I wanted to meet people, take pictures, and learn about the points of interest, both previously identified and those that I spontaneously discovered en route. I also wanted to venture forth only in daylight (with two notable fishy exceptions to be described later). Furthermore, I had to consider the logistics and time required to arrive at each day's starting point and to get home from the ending point. I would use a combination of buses (a remarkably dense and easily navigated network, economical but slow), Uber rides, and driving. Considering all these factors, ten miles a day at one to two miles per hour seemed about right.

I went back to my AAA map and divided the city-limits line into roughly ten-mile intervals. That created 34 segments. Walking two segments weekly would be physically feasible and let me finish in about four to five months accounting for some rainy weather and some away time.

I had 500 business cards and two T-shirts printed with the outline of Los Angeles city limits prominently depicted. That way when I talked to people, I could easily point to the map on my chest and show them where we were standing, where I had come from, and what was in store. They seemed to appreciate having the business card, and I could tell by hits on my blog site, www.lacitylimits.info, that many of these contacts began following my progress.

I chose not to wear headphones or dark glasses because I wanted to be maximally approachable. And I already had plenty of loose belongings to manage. On my head, a baseball cap that simply indicated *Los Angeles*. In my hands: trekking poles. In readily accessible pockets: cell phone, business cards, wallet, and a printout of the day's itinerary. In a small backpack with sewn-on reflective strips: sunblock, hand sanitizer, dry socks, windbreaker, selfie stick, snacks, notebook, hydration bladder (explained below), binoculars, and hand towel.

Trekking poles for an urban walk? Maybe you haven't seen the condition of many of LA's sidewalks—tree roots have lifted numerous sections such that they are impassable by bike and treacherous on foot. Pedestrians often prefer to take their chances and walk in the street. The poles facilitate balance, especially when stepping off and on curbs and over tree roots, particularly important when I was looking ahead and scanning the neighborhood for interesting details.

In addition to helping me negotiate irregular pavement, the poles were great aids on unpaved paths. Seven of the 34 segments are partly or entirely wilderness hikes, and the poles were especially helpful for efficient and safe transit on steep trails, both uphill and down. The same was true for walking on the beach. Sure, a spry dog can hop on its hind legs, but if it wants to really go, it uses all four. Same for me. Finally, the poles gave my shoulders and triceps a bit of a workout, and gripping the poles certainly kept my hands from getting puffy, which happens when I leave them down at my sides for a while. (My wife and

I call this phenomenon "museum hands," which results from them swelling a bit when they dangle without much activity. Or it could be called "airplane feet." If you have ever taken your shoes off on a plane trip and then had trouble fitting your feet back inside on arrival, you understand. Water flows downhill, even inside us.)

Speaking of water, what is a hydration bladder? One brand is CamelBak, which accurately describes this flexible reservoir of drinking water that mountain bikers and runners strap on their backs and sip water through an extension tube while on the go. Mine fits inside my pack. The tube comes out the top, passes over my shoulder, and is within reach of my mouth. Bite the mouthpiece and suck. Voila, thirst is quenched without fumbling to retrieve a water bottle.

My original intent was to walk the entire perimeter alone. That way I could pick my days, start and stop when I felt like it, and be more approachable for conversation with people I met along the way. When I told my wife about my proposed trek, her immediate response was, "You're nuts. If you are not devoured by a mountain lion you will be mugged for your shoes." Friends were equally apprehensive. "Are you taking a Glock?" "Carry a Taser." So to control risk and allay everyone's concerns, I recruited walking companions for certain segments. The first such segments were wilderness trails where hikers sometimes get lost, sprain an ankle, or both, and where cell service is marginal at best, even when glimpses of "civilization" are visible in the distance. The second ones were several urban segments, which by age-old reputation would be considered by many to be unsafe. These areas were in South Los Angeles where the Watts riots (1965) and the Rodney King riots (1992) took place.

Before my walk, I drove my intended route through those urban areas. I saw nothing threatening. I also phoned a senior lead officer for the Los Angeles Police Department about the advisability of an older white man walking through South LA. He said, "You will stand out" and suggested walking when school was in session, staying on main streets, and not displaying any bling. Following that advice and walking with a companion, I felt confident that any risk was minimal and manageable. After all, an adventurist takes pains to minimize risks and confronts others as they arise.

Whatever confidence I had, it was thinly veiled. I had some apprehensions. Would I burn out? Would a knee that had recently pained me for a year hold me back? Were my feet up to it? Would I get bored traversing several stretches of four to six miles where there were no apparent points of interest? Sometimes the planning overwhelmed me. I found myself repeatedly staring at the computer screen and my list of attractions for an hour without deriving an acceptable route on a day of the week when the points of interest would be open. Would my potential walking companions be available and want to join me on the sketchier segments or just on the highly attractive ones?

Then when I was tired, it got worse. "Why am I doing this? It's too hard." "Will anybody be interested in learning about it?" "If they do, will it motivate some readers to get out of their neighborhoods and have a walking adventure of their own?" "Are my observations mundane, irrelevant?"

You decide.

CHAPTER 2

RELICS

Some people disparagingly call my city "La La Land," shorthand, I suppose, that implies superficial, trivial, silly, glitzy, insignificant, fake, infantile, brash, artificial. These outsiders may suggest, if not smugly say, that Los Angeles lacks gravitas, substance, and history. True, no Xian warriors, Egyptian pyramids, or even a North Church, although we do have a full-scale replica of the latter; but in total, how wrong they are.

There is plenty of history here, evident if critics would walk the line with me. I can't claim that doing so provides the complete story, but there are sufficient relics and remnants along the way to gain a good sense of the area's past. Additionally, this eclectic collection of bygones that I encountered are historical biopsies that pay homage to the dreams and accomplishments of the many cultures that have left their mark on the City of Angels. Rather than describing these relics in sequence as I encountered them while walking counterclockwise around the boundary, I would rather place them in a semblance of chronological order, which means we start about 7000 years ago.

A most unlikely surprise in West LA is a two-acre fenced-off area behind University High School and otherwise bounded by low-rise apartment buildings. A sign in the small parking lot indicates Kuruvunga Springs Cultural Center and Museum, Gabrielino Tongva Springs Foundation. The Tongva Indians inhabited the

Southern California region perhaps 8000 years ago, and along with the neighboring Chumash, were the most influential natives at the time of European exploration. When the Spanish arrived in the 18th century and established the San Gabriel Mission, they called the area's Indigenous people Gabrieleños, hence the inclusion of that name on the sign. In the Tongva language, -*nga* means "the place of," and Kuruvunga means "a place where we are in the sun." (Today, well-known place names in Southern California stemming from the Tongva language include Topanga, "a place where the mountain meets the sea" and Cucamonga, "a sandy place.")

Kuruvunga was one of 31 known villages in the region, each including as many as 500 thatched dwellings. The springs at Kuruvunga were a source of fresh water first for the Tongva and later for the Spanish. Gaspar de Portola and his entourage camped at Kuruvunga in 1769 while they were on their way to establish California missions. An accompanying priest remarked that the spring's flowing water reminded him of Santa Monica's tears, and coincidentally, that day was her name day. Later, when the city of Santa Monica's founders heard this story, they named their new city (whose boundary was and is less than a mile away) after the saint. Not long after, engineers channeled the spring's 25,000 gallons of daily flow to supply the city's inhabitants.

Today, because of contamination from urban runoff, the water is diverted into a storm drain and heads for the ocean. Nonetheless, the site is a pocket of tranquility, as the sight of the spring water welling up from the earth seems to transcend time. There is also a towering several-hundred-year-old Mexican cypress tree and an array of native plants that were restored in recent years.

A cultural center displays various artifacts that were found at the site when the high school was built.

Twelve years after de Portola and his entourage camped at Kuruvunga, about 12 miles to the east, 44 settlers founded El Pueblo de Nuestra Señora la Reina de los Ángeles de Porciúncula (*por-si-UN-ku-luh*) (The Town of Our Lady the Queen of the Angels of Porciúncula), which eventually became known by its shorter name— Los Angeles.) The pueblo was sited according to rules documented in the Laws of the Indies, which was the first urban planning guide to reach the Americas. King Phillip II of Spain had issued this guide more than two hundred years earlier. It stipulated that all colonies should be located at least 20 miles from the coast (to discourage piracy) and close to both a source of fresh water (the LA River) and a population of indigenous people (the Tongva village of Yaanga), for labor. The Laws also indicated that the street grid should be turned 45 degrees from the cardinal points on the compass to maximize the benefit of passing breezes.

For reasons unknown, the layout for the streets within this pueblo's square shape, about five miles on an edge, were cocked 36 degrees, and that decision is evident today. Although the pueblo's original size has increased 16 times due to multiple annexations, Indiana Street, on the eastern edge of the original plot, still marks the city limits. Walking north along Indiana, the cross streets on the left veer off to the northwest and southwest according to the Laws of the Indies, while those on the right head directly east according to a later north-south/east-west grid laid out for the remainder of the metropolitan area.

Had the British or Dutch colonized Southern California rather than the Spanish, who were controlled by the Laws of the Indies, the city would have logically been sited where most major cities on earth are—immediately adjacent to a navigable body of water. In LA's case, that would have been 21 miles to the south, where the Los Angeles River, not navigable at most times even by canoes, empties into the ocean at Long Beach. Who knows what they might have named it, but probably not El Pueblo de Nuestra Señora la Reina de los Ángeles de Porciúncula.

Although the original name did not stick, the Spanish Empire's mark on California was vast and included the establishment of 21 missions connecting San Diego to San Francisco by an overland route (later to be known as El Camino Real, The King's Road). In the Los Angeles area these outposts were Mission San Gabriel Arcángel (1771) and Mission San Fernando Rey de España (1797). Neither one was within range for my walk just inside the line, but within my range I looked for two relics related to their construction—lime kilns. I found only one.

From prehistoric times, humans have heated limestone to a high temperature, which converts to lime. It can be mixed with water to make durable floor binders, mortar, and wall coatings, all necessary for presentable colonial missions. The stone kiln is large enough to contain chunks of limestone layered with firewood and to produce the necessary 1600°F temperature for the conversion to occur. For efficiency, kilns were built close to limestone outcroppings, and the two on my route were on the northwest swing through the San Fernando Valley, specifically in El Escorpion Park and in the Chatsworth Nature Preserve.

I spent some time searching for the one in Escorpion Park, traipsing back and forth through waist-high shrubs on the bank of a dry creek. Eventually, I gave up without much reluctance since the photographs I had seen on the internet—a tumbling down arch of stones dug into the hillside—were not impressive.

Evidence of the kiln in the Chatsworth Nature Preserve was obvious from 200 yards away, but it was on the other side of a chain-link fence. All I could see was a sloping metal roof supported by four corner posts. The preserve is open one Sunday each spring, otherwise it is true to its name and preserves nature, a lime kiln, and rainwater, which collects behind a miles-long earthen dam before it seeps into the ground.

A metro stop next to Universal City, home of Harry Potter, now sits practically on top of Campo de Cahuenga (*cah-WING-gah*), which in Tongva means place of the hill or maybe place of the fox. This farmstead was built around 1800 and likely incorporated lime from the same kilns that supplied Mission San Fernando, 12 miles north. The Mission probably used the Campo for its cattle operations.

In 1821, Mexico won its independence from Spain. At the time Mexico comprised not only its current-day area but also all of what is now California, Nevada, Utah, and New Mexico, most of Arizona and Colorado, and parts of Oklahoma, Kansas, and Wyoming. Under new Mexican rule, most restrictions that Spain had imposed on trade were lifted, and American traders, particularly from Boston, quickly dominated California's economy. New England's manufactured goods came west. Cow hides, which supplied the East Coast's shoe industry, went east. (Richard Henry Dana recounts the hide trade in *Two Years Before the Mast*, published in 1840.)

By then, the United States was becoming nervous that a European power would claim California and so offered to purchase it. That failed. War broke out in 1846 over a border dispute and continued until Andrés Pico (*PEE-coh*) realized that his Mexican forces were greatly outnumbered and outgunned and surrendered to the commander of the American forces, John Freemont. The two men met at the Campo early in 1847 and signed a peace agreement—the Capitulation at Cahuenga, thus ending hostilities in California.

After American forces overcame the Mexicans in Mexico City the following year, the treaty of Guadalupe Hildago ended the war and ceded California and the American Southwest to the United States. For the first time, America stretched across the entire continent, made possible by the agreement that was sealed at Campo de Cahuenga. Gold was discovered the same year. California joined the Union two years later. Busy times.

Today, only low foundation remnants of the Campo remain visible. Much more stonework was discovered during excavation for the metro station in the 1990s. These remnants inconveniently extended well under the adjacent busy six-lane Lankershim Boulevard. Conun-

drum: Close the street and leave the remnants of this important historical site exposed, or pave over the foundation and poke history in the eye? Compromise: The stones and lime mortar remain exposed within the modern walls of the historic site. The location of the rest is identified by colored pavers slashing obliquely across the sidewalk and under the wheels of passing drivers, who likely have no clue that here the Manifest Destiny would imminently be realized.

Campo de Cahuenga was one of the points of interest on my trek that stirred my emotions. Had Freemont's forces not prevailed over Pico's, the shape of the United States and the history of California would have been dramatically different.

Not nearly so well concealed as the Campo's foundation, the Old Santa Susana Stage Road is an easily identifiable and approachable remnant. It is not far north of the Chatsworth Nature Preserve, where I had spotted a lime kiln in the distance. The Civil War disrupted the normal stagecoach route between Los Angeles and San Francisco through Tejon Pass, so a new road over the mountains farther west and bordering the San Fernando Valley was built. The first mail passed along this steep road in 1861. Ascending, passengers disembarked and walked, placing stones behind the coach's wheels when the horses needed a rest. Cargo was often divided in half and taken up in two runs. Descending south into the San Fernando Valley was even more challenging and justified the name given to one part of the route, the Devil's Slide. Drivers blindfolded their horses to avoid spooking. and they affixed chains or ropes to the front and rear wheels on each side, which caused the wheels to skid rather than roll. Timbers stuck through the spokes under the chassis served the same purpose. Mercifully, a new, less stress-inducing route was opened in 1895, but ruts in the soft sandstone caused by the skidding wheels are still evi-dent. One can enjoy a nice hike by starting next to the cemetery where Fred Astaire and Ginger Rogers are buried, continuing past an unusual rock formation known as the laby-rinth and a so-called waterfall, and following the ruts up to the Santa Susana Pass to savor a spectacular panorama of the

San Fernando Valley. No blindfolds are needed.

For the flatter parts of Los Angeles, electric trolley cars eventually supplanted horse-drawn conveyances. The trolleys are long gone, but traces of their existence are evident upon scrutiny. Captains of industry in the early 20th century were madly buying up property on the outer limits of Los Angeles, subdividing it, and crisscrossing the entire region with a network of trolley cars, especially the beloved Red Cars operated by the Pacific Electric Railway Company, which in the 1920s became the largest electric railway system in the world.

One historically significant remnant of the Red Car line is a single-story, three-room train station built of wood on land donated in 1902 by Charles Watts, who owned several hundred acres of grazing land in this area south of downtown and hoped to subdivide it for residential development. He knew that good public transportation and a nearby train station would make this neighborhood more attractive.

In due time, Watts Junction became a major stop on the Red Car service between Los Angeles and Long Beach as well as a hub for an interconnecting line to other areas. Working-class families, who depended on the Red Cars for travel, moved in. During the 1940s, Watts became a principally Black community as thousands of African Americans migrated from the segregated South looking for better opportunities. Watts was attractive because it did not have racially restrictive covenants that prevented Black people from settling in most other neighborhoods in Southern California.

Success, however, bred overcrowding, poverty, and crime. When the Long Beach line shut down in 1961, residents were cut off from jobs, shopping, and entertainment in surrounding areas. Resentment grew, especially regarding inadequate schools and hospitals and abusive police practices. It exploded one day in August 1965. Riots ensued for five days and resulted in 34 deaths and the burning of all of the shops for a quarter of a mile on either side of the train station along 103rd Street. That stretch became known as Charcoal Alley.

The train station, though, somehow remained intact throughout the turmoil and then became a symbol of hope and renewal for the community as noted by its inclusion on the National Register of Historical Places in 1974. Today, it is a customer service office for the LA Department of Water and Power, and the adjacent Metro Blue Line provides train service from LA to Long Beach along the old Red Car right of way.

My trek took me along Charcoal Alley, past the train station, and over the railroad tracks through what is now a working-class neighborhood where I had left my car all day, undisturbed. The mention of "Watts" causes hearts of many safety-minded and perhaps overly anxious Angelenos to skip a beat, yet most have never been there. Having walked 30-plus miles through Watts and the rest of South Los Angeles on weekdays, my trekking companion and I felt no apprehension and agreed that the area does not deserve its bad reputation.

Just as it had in Watts, the real estate business boomed in the early 1900s all across LA, and many new homeowners bought cars. Red Car ridership dwindled, and rail service folded. The Red Cars' rights of way, however, linger on. Cutting diagonally across the Ballona (buy-YOH-nah) Wetlands Ecological Preserve, which is a soggy estuary that developers would love to drain and develop, is an earthen bed raised well above high tide. It used to support Red Car tracks carrying passengers from West LA to the beach just north of what would become Los Angeles International Airport.

Identifying other areas of previous electric trolley routes might take a bit more imagination, but anywhere a boulevard seems inordinately expansive or where there is a wide grassy median between the lanes of opposing traffic, a trolley line likely occupied that space. Three examples that I walked along are Vermont Avenue through South LA, San Vicente Boulevard bordering Santa Monica, and Chandler Boulevard in North Hollywood. The latter is graced by a path that takes pedestrians and cyclists past sculptures, murals, exercise equipment, a children's playground, landscaping with park benches, and a fenced-in dog run—all far more aesthetically pleasing than a trolley line.

Those rails and ties have all been removed. However, at the beach near the border between LA and Santa Monica, a ten-foot section of track from another enterprise is the sole remnant of a two-track railroad pier that extended nearly a mile into the ocean. When it was completed in 1894, it was the longest pier in the world and was appropriately called Long Wharf. Recognizing that Los Angeles needed a port to become a great city (and to increase the value of his vast real estate holdings), railroad magnate Collis Huntington had arranged for its construction.

For 20 years, Long Wharf was Port Los Angeles, and Huntington used his considerable financial and political influence to have a breakwater built in Santa Monica Bay to protect Long Wharf (and his interests). He also lobbied to retard the building of a breakwater farther south, one that would protect the competing but shallow-bottomed port at San Pedro (PEE-droh). The breakwater at Long Wharf was not built. The one in San Pedro was. That, along with San Pedro dredging its harbor to accommodate larger ships and becoming annexed to Los Angeles in 1909 led to Long Wharf's obsolescence after about 20 years.

Today, a short section of the Long Wharf track deadends at a

boulder that honors it with a bronze commemorative plaque. Surfers ride the waves near one end of the old track. Cars zip along the Pacific Coast Highway not far from the other.

Dogs have benefited from another dashed dream. George Gordon Whitnall moved to Los Angeles in 1913. He was 25 and quickly saw how haphazardly the region was growing, which risked its prosperity and ultimately its stability. He lobbied for a city planning commission; and once it was established, he became its secretary and sole employee. Whitnall strongly believed that LA would become the most important city on the West Coast and would increasingly suffer from poor transportation without effective oversight. Although city planning was an alien concept to most Angelenos, he managed, with difficulty, to bring about the construction of Sepulveda Boulevard, the Arroyo Seco Parkway, Balboa Boulevard, and the extremely wide San Fernando Boulevard. All of these projects allowed for efficient travel from widely separated areas of the metropolis.

His pet project, however, was the Whitnall Highway, which ran obliquely and made a shortcut across the fully gridded San Fernando Valley. In 1927, a small section was opened, and Whitnall had plans for the rest: an 80-foot-wide central swath for traffic at unlimited speed that was bounded on both sides by 35-foot-wide landscaped parkways, which in turn were bounded on both sides by 45-foot-wide roads for local traffic. The parkways would support towers carrying high-voltage power lines. Homeowners balked, but the land was acquired. Some of their properties were condemned and demolished. Because of the oblique course, other properties had major triangular sections taken away, greatly diminishing their value. The plan stalled and then died. The right of way remained, but the presence of the power lines precluded the development of any permanent structures. This gave rise to the creation of a huge off-leash dog park, by far the largest of any I walked past.

There are four more relics that offer glimpses of the past, but maybe because they are from relatively recent times, they each have an unsettling element.

The first is at the far edge of a grassy picnic area shaded with a scattering of trees in the vast Griffith Park. I followed a trail through the woods to get there. Picnickers could come directly from a parking lot but still would have to walk for five to ten minutes. It is a little remote. Low-hanging branches preclude a panoramic view across the area and shroud the eventual surprise. Spanning perhaps a hundred yards at the far side is an irregular cliff-like rock formation that rises 25 to 30 feet. It is rimmed with slightly overhanging boulders that would make climbing up and over difficult. A dozen shallow caves with irregular ten-foot-tall openings punctuate the cliff at intervals. When I was there, no one was around. The word *foreboding* came to mind. I asked myself, "What's inside?" With some trepidation, I stepped in. There was nothing.

In times gone by, my curiosity could have led to my being mauled by Ivan the Terrible, a 900-pound polar bear, for this was the original site of the LA Zoo. It opened in 1912 with 15 animals, shaky financing, and rudimentary enclosures. In the 1920s, film producer William Selig donated the menagerie of animals he had portrayed in his movies.

The most famous of Selig's animals was Topsy, a Bactrian camel, brought from overseas in the 1850s to serve in the United States Camel

Corps and ferry supplies across Arizona and California desert to the Union Army's outpost in Wilmington, near San Pedro. Subsequently Topsy worked in a mine, survived a train wreck, performed in the Ringling Brothers circus, and starred in movies before spending the last of her roughly 81 years in the LA Zoo. She died in 1934 while the Works Progress Administration was constructing new rock formation enclosures. Walt Disney frequented the zoo, and old photographs show his animators in front of these enclosures sketching the anatomy and movements of the big cats and Ivan the Terrible, hence adding realism to Disney's animated films.

The zoo moved two miles north to its present commodious accommodations in 1966. The fencing around the old enclosures has been removed, leaving the rock formations and an eerie sense that ghosts of animals are crouching in the shadows.

Biggies in the entertainment industry—Cecil B. DeMille, Cary Grant, Gloria Swanson, and Doris Day included—were attracted to the second site, where I felt an eerie sense of the ghosts of our own kind. An upscale housing development called Surfridge was initiated in the 1920s immediately inland from what is now Dockweiler State Beach and above the beach dunes. The area south of Venice was bounded on its inland side by an airport of secondary importance, Mines Field. Over the next several decades, a developer built nearly a thousand custom homes with ocean views. Life for the residents was idyllic even though Mines Field morphed into Los Angeles Municipal Airport in 1930 and later into Los Angeles International Airport (LAX) in 1949. Whereas the privileged residents of Surfridge in 1928 might have wandered over to Mines Field to enjoy the National Air Races, life became progressively less idyllic under the takeoff paths of the ever-more-frequent and larger planes.

The advent of the jet age in the 1950s proved to be the death knell for Surfridge. To facilitate airport expansion and mitigate complaints of jet engine noise, Los Angeles City, the owner of LAX, used its power of eminent domain and forcefully bought out all the homeowners. Some homes were moved, others bulldozed. Traces of the subdivision can be viewed either through a tall chain-link fence or through the window of a plane immediately after liftoff. The post-apocalyptic remnants are the streets, curbs, sidewalks, and retaining walls, now with weed- and shrub-filled cracks. A few scruffy palm trees punctuate the barren landscape. On a bright note, endangered El Segundo blue butterflies and burrowing owls have taken up residence in this now-gated community (or gated non-community) and are not apparently fazed by jet engine noise.

The core of Orcutt Ranch, now a city park, is in the West Hills neighborhood of LA's San Fernando Valley. It includes several eye-opening relics. William Orcutt was a petroleum geologist and pioneer in the development of the oil industry in California. He collected fossils of saber-toothed tigers, ground sloths, and dire wolves from the La Brea Tar Pits and alerted the scientific community to the importance of these finds. Orcutt owned a ranch and an orange grove in the San Fernando Valley and built a vacation home there in 1920s, by which time water from the faraway Owens Valley (details in Chapter 3) would have been irrigating his fields and orchards. It was the architect's and Orcutt's interest in the historic styles and symbols of the American Southwest that led them to build a one-story ranch house with a central courtyard and fountain, thick stucco walls, and a clay tile roof. Nothing unusual there. But as a recurring embellishment above doors and windows as well as elsewhere on the property, they used the swastika motif repeatedly.

An explanation is in order, and it is forthcoming on a sign in the parking lot, so visitors have clarification before they have any opportunity to be offended. Predating ancient Egypt, the swastika is one of the world's oldest and most widely distributed graphic symbols across all the inhabited continents. The word swastika comes from Sanskrit and meant "well-being," "good fortune," and "luck." For centuries, Native Americans have woven swastikas, which they independently derived, into their blankets and applied them to their jewelry for centuries, so it is not surprising that it became part of the ranch's embellishment. In the 1930s, the Nazis adopted this symbol and invested it with an aura of hate and intimidation. At the Orcutt Ranch, the presence of swastikas, while understandable, is unsettling.

Several trees on the property also have a place in history. Creekside, near the park's rear boundary, an ancient and badly misshapen oak tree struggles for its survival, but it has been succeeding at this for perhaps 700 years. It is the oldest tree in Los Angeles and likely the ugliest. That is not the tree's fault, however, because its present form is the hacked-up result of generations of settlers removing large sections of it to fuel the lime kiln at Mission San Fernando, 10 miles away.

Finally, recall that Orcutt had an orange grove. On the property midway between the house and the creek, I saw a rusted tower of

uncertain age and stability that was topped with two automobile-size gasoline engines only partially enclosed in collapsing wooden housings. A five-foot weathered airplane propeller was attached to each motor. In their prime, they kept the chilly night air moving and prevented frost from forming on the orange blossoms. Within fan range of the props stood several scraggly chest-high citrus trees, which were nearly as ill-formed as their oak cousin down by the creek. Each one supported only sparse foliage and enough oranges for a glass of juice. A large modern sign in bold black lettering shouted Do NOT PICK THE FRUIT. I am uncertain whether "fruit" in this instance was a singular or plural noun. I hope the grove looked better in Orcutt's time.

I had read about the Old LA Zoo, Surfridge, and the Orcutt Ranch before I went to see them. By contrast, I stumbled on the fourth eerie relic completely by chance. My reaction was the same as when I see an item from my childhood that is for sale in an antique store. "Whoa, am I that old?"

This shocker was at the corner of Rosecrans and Vermont in South LA. An open-front metal box about 18 inches wide and 3 feet tall stood on a post at eye level. Badly weathered lettering across the top faintly revealed its identity: Phone.

A pay phone! Even the handset and the cord were there. I was skeptical that it was working. I had to try it. Several quarters later, I was talking to my wife, 20 miles away. "Hello?" "You'll never guess where I'm calling from."

Like Watts Station, the final relic I discovered also has official historical recognition, this time from the City of Los Angeles. The bronze plaque declares,

OTOMISAN RESTAURANT
ESTABLISHED 1956 IN BOYLE HEIGHTS.
OLDEST CONTINUOUSLY OPERATING JAPANESE RESTAURANT IN
THE CITY OF LOS ANGELES.

Foodie friends Amy and Phil picked up my wife, drove to the restaurant east of downtown, and met me there at the end of that day's ten-mile walking segment for an early dinner. I thought we should be there when it opened because I had read that it was small and that later there would be a line.

Yes, indeed, small and quaint. Three booths for four diners each lined one wall. The other wall was the "back bar" with a TV, rice cooker, and refrigerator. A low counter ran down the middle of the room fronted by five barstools, four covered in brown vinyl, one in red. Assorted Japanese memorabilia further contributed to the homey ambiance.

In the early 20th century, Boyle Heights and Watts were two of only a few neighborhoods that did not have restrictive housing covenants banning non-white residents. So Jewish, Japanese, and Mexican immigrants settled in Boyle Heights along with many others from Yugoslavia, Russia, and Armenia. The mixed ethnicity of the neighborhood changed for three reasons—in response to many Japanese Americans being forced into internment camps during World War II, the construction of a gigantic network of highway interchanges that divided the neighborhood, and "redlining" by local banks that made home loans hard to obtain. Those who could afford homes found it easier to move away than to obtain a loan to buy a home in Boyle Heights. Now the neighborhood is principally Hispanic, but Otomisan remains.

The food was the traditional menu found in most Japanese restaurants. I hope the restaurant remains sufficiently popular for the owners to stay in business as long as they wish, if for nothing more than to preserve an important part of LA's history of ethnic diversity.

I opened this chapter with a description of a most ancient relic, the Kuruvunga Springs. Water was then and remains a crucial component of LA's history and deserves a chapter of its own.

CHAPTER 3

WATER

Southern California is renowned for its mild climate and blue skies. The dirty secret is that the city's greenness is contrived because we receive on average only 15 inches of rain annually. Unless you are a gardener or farmer that may not mean anything, so here is some perspective. The average annual rainfall across the United States is about 30 inches a year, ranging from 62 inches in Miami and New Orleans (way too much for me) to less than 3 inches in Yuma, Arizona (drier than many deserts).

All other US cities receive more than Yuma. New York and Houston each receive 50 inches, Chicago 37. All of them are green, but NYC and Chicago can be bitterly cold; Houston, unbearably hot. Temperature extremes in LA are generally not an issue, but limited rainfall and year-to-year variation have always been. We can go for five to seven years averaging less than 10 inches of rain, and one recent year brought only 3 inches to the parched City of Angels. Even when it does rain, it all arrives between November and April, and it often comes so fast that much of it runs into the ocean before soaking in. Then too, the engineers have paved multiple waterways to hasten the rain's departure and minimize the risk of flooding.

So, you rightfully ask, "What does this climate report have to do with walking the line?" Everything. Water has been the main determinant in LA's weird shape, more so than the discovery of oil nearby, the discovery of gold up north, or the development of the entertainment industry. Hence, water dictated my rambling's course.

Native Americans inhabited the area perhaps 8000 years ago and relied on naturally flowing springs and seasonal flow in the streams and rivers for their water needs. When the Spanish established colonies in the 18th century, they were required by the king's edict to site their pueblos next to a source of fresh water *and* at least 20 miles from the coast, hence the inland location of the original city, established in 1781. It enclosed a square about 5 miles on a side, which was plenty of room for the original 14 families consisting of 44 individuals.

Over the ensuing years, Mexico won its independence from Spain (1821), California won its independence from Mexico (1848), and California joined the Union (1850). During that time, LA's city limits expanded considerably beyond the original square as city leaders championed grand ideas. Then the boundaries contracted as the interests of peeved, independently minded ranch owners prevailed in court. At the time of its centennial celebration in 1871, Los Angeles was only one square mile larger than it had been originally, which did not say much for any enduring efforts of the early empire builders. The next 60 years would be remarkably different and make the city far larger and longer to walk around.

First came five annexations in the 1890s that added 14 square miles to the city, but they did not dramatically change its shape. Residents in the annexed areas voted themselves in to benefit from public services provided by Los Angeles, but by doing so they gave up a degree of independence. Los Angeles welcomed them because they increased the city's tax base.

Then in 1906 everything went wonky. For several decades prior, various power brokers had competed to establish either Santa Monica or San Pedro/Wilmington as Los Angeles's port. San Pedro/Wilmington dredged their waterway to make their wharves immediately available to ocean-going ships and won out. Then both LA and Long Beach were thirsting to annex those cities to markedly increase their tax base without having to greatly expand public services. Long Beach had the advantage because it shared a boundary with both San Pedro and Wilmington.

Los Angeles was vexed because state law mandated that any territory that a city annexed had to be in contact with the existing city limits. In other words, no whimsical "island" annexations. Alas, the closest boundary of LA was 12 miles to the north, and LA did not particularly want to annex the intervening areas (Torrance, Gardena, Carson, Willowbrook) because the cost of providing city services to them would outweigh any gain in tax revenue. So in 1906, and in anticipation of eventually bringing San Pedro and Wilmington into its fold, LA annexed a strip of property that in places was no wider than a half mile but that brought LA's border in contact with San Pedro and Wilmington. The strip was (and is) known as "The Shoestring," but at that moment nothing was dangling from its end.

The harbor cities were not enamored with the prospect of being tied to the end of a shoestring and overpowered by landlubber LA, whose corporate interests were generally hostile to those of the harbor's multitude of union workers. Los Angeles promised better fire and police services, reliable rubbish removal, electric streetlights, better schools, and improved water and sewers. Furthermore, the harbor cities knew that they did not have the financial resources for the improvements needed to develop a world-class port on their own. In 1909, the voters in Wilmington cast 107 ballots in favor of annexation, 61 against. A week later, the vote in San Pedro was 726 pro, 227 con.

Opposition in LA was scant. The area of Los Angeles jumped from 43 square miles to 76. More importantly and for the first time, Los Angeles had a bona fide seaport, even if it could not quite call itself a seaport city. From my perspective, these annexations greatly increased the length of my walk yet made it far more interesting.

Navigable water had another major influence on the mad growth of Los Angeles seen in the early 20th century. It conveyed cargo ships rapidly between the Atlantic and Pacific Oceans via the Panama Canal, which opened in 1914. As a result of this expedited trade route, Los Angeles benefited grandly in size, wealth, and census, except for one problem—the dearth of fresh water for its rapidly growing population.

Beginning just a few years earlier, a self-taught civil engineer, William Mulholland, gradually worked his way up from laborer to superintendent of the Los Angeles Water Department. He recognized LA's potential to become a world-class city if a reliable source of freshwater could quench the thirst of the growing population. The water could also irrigate vast expanses of scruffy grazing land and convert it into profitable farms growing fruits and vegetables. Mulholland set his eye on the Owens Valley, over 200 miles to the north. Via a proposed engineering and construction project equal to that of the Panama Canal, he put forward the idea that melted snow from the eastern slopes of the Sierra Nevada Mountains, which would normally drain into the Owens Valley and nurture local farms, could be diverted into an aqueduct and guided downhill nearly 4000 feet. The proposal came at a time when LA's annual rainfall for three years in a row averaged less than seven inches, far below the longer-term average of 15.

With the drought on their mind, by a ten-to-one margin, Angelenos approved a $1 million bond election in 1905 to develop a plan and a $23 million bond issue two years later to build the aqueduct. In 1913, Owens Valley water first tumbled down the Cascades into the San Fernando Valley near LA amidst great fanfare.

On one hand, Mulholland achieved God-like status for carrying this scheme to a successful conclusion. Conversely, some chicanery was involved in duping Owens Valley farmers out of their nearby water supply and in convincing Angelenos that their existing supply was far more meager than it was. (A fictionalized version of this story was dramatized in the movie *Chinatown* released in 1974.)

Since Los Angeles financed the aqueduct, it was going to control who the beneficiaries were, and this reality added greatly to LA's contorted shape. Surrounding cities and unincorporated areas had a difficult choice—remain independent and arid, or vote to join the behemoth, contribute to the paydown of the aqueduct's construction debt, and share the new water supply. After Wilmington and San Pedro acquiesced in 1909, 73 other entities followed over the next quarter century, losing their independence and some of their identity.

This process became markedly easier when the California legislature passed the Annexation Act of 1913. Now LA voters did not have to approve the annexation, just the voters in the area under consideration. This obviated special elections that were proving to be expensive and bothersome for Angelenos. It also led to smaller areas being acquired, at times no larger than a pocket of residential lots. Furthermore, the boundaries delineating any proposed annexation could be easily gerrymandered to include voters who were in favor and exclude those who were against, which further contributed to the jagged city outline. In 1914, J.M. Guinn in *The Annual Publication of the Historical Society of Southern California* wrote of LA's shape, "... there is no geometric term that will describe its shape. There is no living thing with which it can be compared."

It got worse.

Readers familiar with Southern California will recognize the names of other areas that signed up for water. Largest of them all, the San Fernando Valley annexation in 1915 added a whopping 170 square miles, which more than doubled LA's area. Others, all much smaller, included Palms (1915), Chatsworth (1920), Sawtelle (1922), Eagle Rock (1923), Lankershim (1923), Fairfax (1924), Santa Monica Canyon (1925), Tuna Canyon (1926), White Point (1928), and Tujunga (1932).

Barnes City was a special case and provides a far more colorful story of annexation than just caving in for water. Venice, a seaside resort town, incorporated in 1905 and welcomed Al Barnes and his wild animal circus and zoo to its beachside location. His attractions conveniently provided entertainment and brought a flood of visitors who Barnes hoped would buy residential property from him. The show was popular, and Barnes expanded it into a circus that toured the country on railroad cars. Venice remained its headquarters and winter home.

Eventually much of the growing population not affiliated with Barnes' enterprises became tired of the noise and disorder, so in 1920 Barnes moved to a nearby ranch, which was wedged between Venice, Mar Vista, and Culver City. Movie studios in Culver City took advantage of the conveniently located zoo and rented Barnes' elephants and monkeys for their productions. Barnes subdivided part of this property, sold residential lots, and sought to incorporate his holdings to protect his circus and zoo from being annexed by outsiders who wanted to curtail his activities.

The vote for incorporation was favorable, but resident homeowners who did not work for Barnes claimed that the election was rigged and that many of the circus and zoo employees who voted were transients and did not live in Barnes City. Lore has it that on election day Barnes arranged the circus schedule so that his monkeys could vote from their cages. Upset residents insisted on a new election, which was denied by Barnes' hand-picked board of directors and mayor, who was Barnes' brother.

Ultimately the homeowners prevailed before the California Supreme Court, who ordered Barnes City to de-incorporate. Santa Monica, Culver City, and Los Angeles competed to annex this newly available territory. All residents who were not circus or zoo employees chose LA.

A new election was held in the summer of 1926 when the circus was out of California on tour. Barnes sent 200 workers back to sway the annexation initiative, but most were unregistered and could not vote. Annexation was approved. The shape of Los Angeles changed once again.

Walking past the area, I tried to imagine hearing the lions roar as they were being fed, as that was one of the neighbors' biggest complaints. I wondered if some of their ire might have been directed at the annoying sounds of the calliope whose player had had an affair with Barnes. He had refused to marry her, and she shot and killed herself on the steps of his Pullman car. Ultimately, Barnes moved his circus and zoo out of town. Barnes City, despite its colorful history, disappeared from the map.

Spanning 23 years between San Pedro and Wilmington joining LA in 1909 and Tujunga in 1932, LA swelled from 76 to 450 square miles, but then in the next 90 years, over 200 additions, reorganizations, and detachments accounted for only 53 square miles of additional area. In other words, the annexation frenzy was over. One reason was that municipalities in Southern California banded together and developed other sources of imported water and were no longer held hostage by LA to supply this precious commodity.

Land surveys today are aided by lasers that are precise to within small fractions of an inch for distance measurements and not to degrees, not to minutes, but to seconds ($1/3600^{th}$ of a degree) for angular measurement. The old Spanish and Mexican property lines must have made later surveyors, developers, and landowners roll their eyes.

J.M. Guinn, quoted above regarding LA's shape, gave some examples. "Commencing at a point in the Angeles River; thence southerly thirty-one hundred and fifty varas more or less; thence westerly sixty-two hundred varas more or less to a nopalera (cactus patch); thence northerly thousand varas more or less to a calera (lime kiln) then easterly seven thousand one hundred varas more or less to the place of beginning."

He also found that early deeds recorded boundary landmarks such as "aguaje de Mocobenga (the mucky spring), the aguaje de Sancito (the spring of the Little Sycamore) and the Portecuelo (little pocket or valley)." Compare that to the precision with which boundaries have subsequently been identified.

Here is a snippet from the five-and-a-half-page, single-spaced, typewritten description of the San Fernando annexation in 1915. "…thence north 72 degrees 9 minutes 50 seconds east, a distance of 333.20 feet to the hereinbefore mentioned northwesterly corner of Lot 1068 of said Tract No. 1000, said point being also the southwesterly corner of Lot "C", the Rancho El Escorpion as per map recorded in Book 4232, pages 124 and 125 of Deeds, Records of said county…" Sounds about right to me.

After I learned about the idiosyncratic lumpiness of Los Angeles, I discovered that such a crazy city outline was by no means unique. Rochester, New York, has a narrow extension that makes it a port city on Lake Ontario. Chicago is a rather orderly rectangle except for a westward blister of property connected by a narrow strip. This brought O'Hare International Airport into the Windy City's clutches. In 2022, in an article titled "Why American Cities Are So Weirdly Shaped," *The Economist* concluded, "With some exceptions, these boundaries are administrative confections that make few allowances for geography, population density or common sense." Now when I make a wrong turn, I would like Siri to tell me, "Go back. You are the victim of an administrative confection."

Mulholland was revered and feted for his accomplishment in turning Los Angeles green and prosperous (never mind that its outline was ziggy). Although power brokers at the time profited grandly from buying up arid tracts, subdividing them, and extending rail and trolley lines in to make them accessible for new residents, Mulholland apparently did not care about or share in any monetary gain brought about by supplying these areas with water. His reputation was sullied a bit by his participation in two deceptions that involved bilking the Owens Valley farmers out of their water and persuading LA's citizens that the aqueduct was absolutely necessary for the city's survival. But he truly fell from his pedestal later in the wake of the disastrous failure of a dam for which he had overseen design, construction, and inspection.

Located north of Los Angeles, it was intended to be an ancillary source of water for the thirsty city. It was completed in 1926, and within months it began to leak. Mulholland and his assistant chief engineer Harvey Van Norman deemed the cracks inconsequential. How wrong they were. Within 12 hours after Mulholland and Van Norman had inspected the dam in 1928 and noted that repairs were needed but were not urgent, the dam failed catastrophically. Twelve billion gallons of water created a wave over 100 feet high as it raced down the canyon. At least 431 people died, and towns below the dam suffered extensive damage. An inquest concluded that an error in engineering judgment and errors in public policy were responsible for the failure but that Mulholland should not be held criminally responsible. Remarkably, Mulholland assumed complete blame for the engineering failure, was devastated by the tragedy, and spent the remainder of his life in relative seclusion.

Several features along LA's boundary memorialize both Van Norman and Mulholland, best appreciated from wilderness vantage points.

Let's take a hike.

CHAPTER 4

NATURE

Except for Juneau, Los Angeles is the tallest city in the United States, measuring in elevation from sea level along the coast at Pacific Palisades, Venice, and San Pedro to 5075 feet high atop Mt. Lukens, 23 miles inland. This peak is in the far northeast corner of the San Fernando Valley and just barely inside the Los Angeles city limits. You could almost kick a rock off the summit into Angeles National Forest.

Mt Lukens's profile is far from iconic, only rarely covered with snow, and whatever natural beauty it might have is marred by an array of communication towers that dominate the summit. It does not get much respect. Most Angelenos have never heard of it. Nonetheless, it seemed like the logical place to begin my counterclockwise 342-mile walk around the Los Angeles city limits.

The first five miles, however, didn't count, because that was the distance from the trailhead at the edge of a residential area up a steep trail through chaparral to the summit. As we ascended, canyons and ridges dropped away with breathtaking steepness in multiple directions, and the closest signs of human endeavor were vast swaths of concrete pavement lining the outlets of the largest canyons far below. These are "catchment basins" designed to protect the adjacent residential neighborhoods from torrents of muddy water and debris that threaten the foothills during the rainy season.

At the summit, Pasadena was visible in the distance to the southeast, and downtown LA was silhouetted to the south. Farther to the south and about 35 miles away, the skyline of downtown Long Beach, just outside the LA city limits, was contrasted against the shimmering Pacific Ocean. Twenty-five miles beyond that, Catalina Island's outline is faintly visible. It was a spectacular panorama, which, for a moment, dissolved any trepidations about the jaunt.

My hiking buddy, Thomas, and I enjoyed the vista, aired out our hiking shoes, and shared what we knew about Theodore Lukens (1848-1918). Foremost, Lukens was a forester and conservationist. While employed by the Forest Service he established a nursery for more than 60,000 experimental tree seedlings, many of which were transplanted in the nearby mountains and in Griffith Park (the topic of Chapter 9). Lukens and John Muir were friends and worked together to promote forest conservation and restoration and the newly formed Sierra Club. Lukens was also a civic leader who served two terms as mayor of nearby Pasadena. The Forest Service gave Mt. Lukens its name in the 1920s.

Thomas and I put our shoes back on, took pictures of each other with the city skyline in the background, and then started walking the line—about six miles via another slightly less steep trail back to civilization. We chose it because it approximated the LA city limits. Along the way, the trail branched multiple times. None of the branch points were marked with more than a steel post, some not at all. Thomas, a more experienced California-wilderness hiker than I, was comfortable with such limited directional guidance, and with the help of the AllTrails app, we made it down with only a few wrong turns, to which AllTrails quickly alerted us. It was good that Thomas had downloaded the app and map, because even with civilization visible in the distance and with multiple communication towers looming above us, cell phone service was intermittent.

Portions of our path down were on fire roads suitable for four-wheel-drive vehicles, and we met a few intrepid mountain bikers and several hikers, some with their dogs. Other portions were narrow tracks with vegetation so close that it snagged our hiking poles with every swing. The worst part, however, was the multitude of fist-sized rocks that were annoyingly located wherever I planted a foot. I was never sure whether to try to step around them or balance on top of them. I don't remember which technique I was attempting to do when I slipped and fell sideways across my trekking pole, snapping its aluminum shaft. But maybe it broke my fall sufficiently that I ended up with only a few knee and elbow scuffs. (Later, at home, I employed my orthopedic skills to repair the broken pole. It no longer collapses for storage, but it is as stout and supportive as before.)

At the end of that trek, we were six miles down, with 336 to go. The spectacular panorama from the top has stayed in my mind—it was a good way to start this adventure.

For the next two days, I was sore, not from the fall, but from delayed onset muscle soreness in my calves. Despite having trained beforehand on seriously steep trails and streets in my neighborhood, my calves were not conditioned for the nearly 3000-foot descent from summit to trailhead. Some people toss around the acronym DOMS when discussing delayed onset muscle soreness as if that makes them sound knowledgeable. They aren't. Nobody is. I will put my orthopedic-surgeon hat on for a minute.

A buildup of lactic acid is a frequently implicated culprit; and muscle contractions do produce lactic acid, but it is metabolized in an hour. DOMS typically does not develop for another day or two. It most often occurs when a muscle repeatedly gets longer rather than shorter while it is trying to contract, which may sound confusing. Consider, for instance, performing an elbow curl while holding a dumbbell. Your biceps contracts, and the dumbbell comes up to your shoulder. Now lower the weight slowly. The biceps is still firing, but it lengthens slowly and allows the elbow to straighten. The calf muscles do the same thing with downhill walking.

Not only is the cause of DOMS unclear, so is the best treatment. Anecdotal advice abounds regarding the purported benefit of ice, heat, foam rolling, massage, light exercise, and herbal preparations. None of the treatments are supported by good science. Time heals all wounds, and once the DOMS-affected muscle recovers, it is resistant to a repeat bout, at least for a while.

The next segment took me west on a residential street that traversed Mt. Luken's foot. The homes on the right had wilderness just beyond their back fences, so it didn't surprise me that wildlife sightings were common. One man pulling out of his driveway indicated that deer and owls were frequent visitors and that he saw a peacock from time to time. Who knows where it escaped from. A dog walker I was chatting with mentioned that he quite often saw coyotes and bobcats in the area and occasionally spotted a bear foraging in trash cans.

Confirming the possibility of bear encounters, California Department of Fish and Wildlife posters stapled to utility poles on street corners warned, "Take action now to secure bear attractants." They itemized steps under the categories of trash and garbage, fruit trees, chickens and beehives, pet food, gardens, compost, homes, and vehicles along with wild bird seed and hummingbird feeders ("Remove or use only in winter when bears are typically less active.").

Then I encountered the first "by the way" on my journey. These were unanticipated discoveries, unseen or at least markedly underappreciated by those zipping past in cars. This "by the way" confirmed the dog walker's observation and the Fish and Wildlife departmental warning. Fairgrove Avenue had recently been coated with a slurry of asphalt to seal the cracks, and before the coating had dried, a car had driven along leaving its tire track. Nothing special about that. But next to the tread marks were the clear footprints of a bear that had padded along for half a block. Later that day, I mentioned this sighting to somebody, and he asked, "Was it a black bear?" I told him that I didn't see the bear but was rather certain that it at least had black feet.

I had divided my trek into 34 segments of roughly 10 miles each. Seven of these I called "wilderness" segments, because even though urban development was often visible in the distance, these were bona fide hikes on trails and fire roads, worthy of hiking boots to blunt the pressure of stepping on sharp rock edges and to provide ankle support. Trekking poles, which I used on the entire trip, were particularly helpful in negotiating steep ascents and descents and trails with uneven and unstable surfaces.

Mt. Lukens is in the extreme northeast corner of Los Angeles, O'Melveny Park is in the extreme northwest corner, about 16 miles away in the Granada Hills neighborhood. The park is the second largest in Los Angeles after Griffith Park and is named after Henry O'Melveny, a distinguished lawyer and an original member of the California State Parks Commission. His son bought the land and bequeathed it to the city in the 1970s.

My day in O'Melveny Park started with a bird sit. Rather than hiking or walking to look for birds, the sit, a monthly event sponsored by the San Fernando Valley Audubon Society, requires five steps. Find a spot, have a seat, wake up your senses, tune into the birds, repeat. Ten birders stood around a picnic table and shared their journal entries since they had last met. We then dispersed across the groomed portion of the park, notebooks and colored pencils in hand, binoculars on the ready. The philosophy is that sketching what you see makes you look more closely. Artists are forever doing that in museums. I found a spot and took a seat on the grass.

It was a beautiful morning—brisk, blue sky, scattered clouds, but no birds. A nearby gopher nudged dirt crumbles out of its burrow with its nose and eyed me warily. I eyed him back. Maybe that woke up my senses, because for the next 45 minutes, I couldn't watch a bird long enough to make good observations and sketch it before another one showed up for review.

Then we reassembled at the picnic table, displayed our notebooks, and shared our observations. Several of the sitters were excellent artists. My drawings were primitive but adequate for one of the experienced birders to identify by name the birds I had seen and sketched— Dark-Eyed Junco, Spotted Towhee, Crow, Western Bluebird, maybe a flycatcher, and the accurately named Yellow-Rumped Warbler. I learned that its not-so-nice nickname is "butter butt."

Thomas and I then took off to summit Mission Point, the highest point in the park and skirting LA's northwesternmost boundary. The AllTrails app rated the trail as difficult, and although it was hardpacked and wide, it was as steep as our previous ascent on Mt. Lukens, but shorter. We gained 1200 feet in elevation before reaching the "Point," which is a misnomer, but it sounds better than Mission Mound or Mission Round Top. Regardless, the view looking southeast across the San Fernando Valley was spectacular. In the far distance, 25 miles away, the downtown LA skyscrapers indicated just how far the city had expanded in this direction since its founding.

In the near distance was the Van Norman Reservoir where water, recently arrived from the Owens Valley via Mulholland's aqueduct, was waiting to serve the city.

But wait, the water looked black. Oh, okay. Thomas and I recalled that 96 million black balls, plastic and about four inches in diameter, cover the surface and reduce evaporation. One can get a glimpse of this unusual covering when driving south on the I-5. It is on the right and goes by fast. The far better view is the bird's eye one from Mission Point.

The third wilderness segment was a little farther south and west. Rimming the San Fernando Valley—Stoney Point Park and Garden of the Gods, across Topanga Canyon Boulevard from each other—are aggregations of gigantic and dramatic sandstone outcroppings that just shout, "The Great American West." In fact, hundreds of grade B westerns were filmed here between 1912 and the late 1960s. The area earned its moniker as the "most shot up location in movie history." Name your favorite cowboy actor from yesteryear, and it is likely that he got shot here (on film) while riding through on his favorite horse. John Wayne, Gene Autry, William Boyd (a.k.a. Hopalong Cassidy), Gary Cooper, Tom Mix, Roy Rogers. From an adjacent residential street, a famous outcropping is evident—the

Lone Ranger Rock. Silver, with actor Clayton Moore astride, would rear up, paw its front feet in the air, and whinny. Then, "Hi ho, Silver. Away!"

This was also where the Joads in the movie *Grapes of Wrath* (1940) got their first glimpse of their new life in the fertile San Fernando Valley.

Walking through the Garden of the Gods is not at all strenuous. Rock hopping through the boulder-strewn Stoney Point Park is a little more so, and paths crisscross everywhere, so it is easy to get turned around. The park is small, however, and it is usually teeming with rock climbers and boulderers, who can help anybody regain their bearings.

Continuing counterclockwise around LA's border, the next photogenic wilderness area I encountered was Chatsworth Park South, where hiking buddies Thomas and Carl and I explored the Old Santa Susana Stage Road. It is listed on the National Register of Historic Places and was the main stagecoach route from LA to San Francisco beginning in 1861. The trip took three days, and likely the most memorable (terrifying?) part was the steep section known as Devil's Slide, which I described in Chapter 1 ("Relics"), because the wheel gouges in the sandstone are still evident. The road remained open and maintained until the late 1800s for local ranchers and farmers, but a railroad connection between LA and San Francisco began service in 1876.

Thomas, Carl, and I all remarked that nowadays the road, which was an entirely passable hiking trail, would be entirely unsuited for any wheeled conveyance. We assumed that imported and compacted soil had made the road somewhat even but now had been washed away, leaving crevices a foot deep and running every which way in the stony substrate.

On our way down from the pass we sought two points of interest we had identified on the map—a waterfall and a labyrinth. We found the waterfall, which was another misnomer. Yes, there was water, and following the dictates of gravity, it was falling. Despite recent rains, however, it was a trickle at best. I guess naming an attraction on the map as a water trickle or a water drip would not pique the interest of potential visitors. That was disappointing, but less so than the fact that we could not find the labyrinth. There is sparse signage in all these parks, which adds not only an element of adventure but also one of frustration.

Once home, I scrutinized blown-up aerial photos, topographical maps, and hikers' descriptions to zero in on the labyrinth's location. So armed, Carl and I went back two weeks later and found it. I wonder if long ago this natural rock formation, nestled in the middle of a broad valley among wildflowers, started as a single massive chunk, which split apart along vertical fault lines and whose sharp edges weathered away over time. What is left, best seen standing on top ten feet up, is a stone maze with clefts inches to feet wide that extend to the ground. It is as if there were fifteen variously sized marshmallows arranged randomly in a shallow pan that had room for twenty. It is an easy walk from the trailhead.

El Escorpion Park is six miles south of the labyrinth along the mountains that define the western border of the San Fernando Valley and LA's city limits. This hike was without a doubt the most unpleasant segment of my entire trek. I may have been lulled by the fact that El Escorpion was another city park, like O'Melveny and Stoney Point, where the hikes were a little strenuous but pleasantly so, i.e., a walk in the park. Google Maps indicated two interesting features in El Escorpion, a peak and a cave. I asked myself, "Where other than LA could there be a cave inside city limits? I've gotta see it." AllTrails described a 2.4-mile loop with an elevation gain of 700 feet. Easy peasy.

The summit is Castle Peak, which with squinting and imagination seems like an appropriately descriptive name, much more so than Mission Point's so-called point. Castle Peak's name, however, is a corruption of the Chumash Indian word *Kas'ele'ew*, meaning tongue. (With even more imagination, the rounded rocky prominence might vaguely resemble a large, lumpy tongue sticking up.) A village at the base of *Kas'ele'ew* was a meeting and trading place between the Chumash, who generally lived farther north and closer to the coast, and the Tongva people, who called the entire San Fernando Valley, El Escorpion, and surrounding areas home.

The Cave of Munits is named for a shaman, who got caught up in a death-avenging scheme and ended up dying a violent death himself on Castle Peak. The grieving mother of the child whose death Munits was supposed to vindicate retreated into a canyon and turned to stone. The canyon's name is Tujunga, tuxúnga in Tongva—old woman's place.

My first attempt to reach the cave and then continue to the peak occurred about a week after a decent rain, and the trail was still muddy. The trekking poles went down and would only pop out with a tug.

Same for feet. We could see a dark vertical cleft in an intensely pocked rock face ahead and knew that the cave was a chimney cave, so we slogged on toward its base. Then the trail narrowed and turned steep, enough so that some lovely person had hacked out boot-sized pockets to step in.

The surface turned from sticky to slick. Thomas and I prevailed and reached the foot of the cave. Shafts of light streamed down from high in the cleft and illuminated a large, generally vertically oriented cavern where eons of erosion had carved side rooms, sluices, and pockets, several of which would have served Munits well as a roost. We knew from the guidebook that climbing up the cave and out of the top was a hands-and-feet scramble not requiring any technical skills or equipment, but that day the rock was wet and slick, so we headed home.

I returned a month later with my other hiking buddy, Carl. (Thomas was busy.) The trail was now dry, and except for having to step around a multitude of deep footprints in the caked mud, we arrived at the base of the cave with remarkable ease. Somebody had left a fixed rope draped over a huge boulder defining the entry, and using this as an assist, I climbed in. Worth the effort. A little challenging, a little risky, a little uncertainty—but that's what defines an adventure.

We then pressed on to the ridge line several hundred feet above the top of the chimney. Here the going got tough—steep and no defined trail, rather a spiderweb of quasi-paths, maybe made by rabbits. If so, they were certainly sure-footed, because the underfooting was nothing but loose gravel.

We finally made it to the ridge and found a real trail headed toward Castle Peak, but we had to clamber down a four-foot ledge to access it. Then it really was a walk in the park to reach CP, climb up, and enjoy a panoramic view of the San Fernando Valley. Looking down from the horizon, we could see the groomed portion of the park 700 feet below and perhaps a mile in the distance.

Then the march from hell began.

We may have missed the trail to complete the loop back to the trailhead; but if we did, so had others. According to accounts on the internet I read later, previous hikers had experienced the same—an adventure gone sour. I don't think anybody descended via the exact route Carl and I took; otherwise, we might have seen some fragments of clothing snagged on branches, epidermis-streaked rocks, and skid marks left by a variety of body parts that do not generally come in contact with the ground on a hike. In some instances, there were suggestions of a path, all filled with gravel and small shrubs.

I couldn't understand why all the rubble had not already tumbled down the steep slopes. Rather, the loose rocks seemed to be waiting to lubricate our descent.

It was infuriating to struggle and yet see the fire road down below where families with their dogs were having amiable Sunday strolls. I supposed that if one of us had broken an ankle, waving and hollering might have drawn attention. It would have been impossible for paramedics to carry somebody out of there on a stretcher or for a helicopter to land. Our phones wouldn't have been helpful because there was no cell service. Also, Carl's popped out of his pocket during a tumble, and he didn't realize it until possibly a hundred skids later. Neither of us wanted to prolong our adventure (more than just a little challenging, risky, and uncertain) to look for it. We survived. Perhaps Munits had cast a favorable spell over us.

Before returning to the peak of Mt. Lukens at the end of the circuit, one wilderness segment remained. I had previously hiked portions of it and scrutinized accounts of the remaining portions on the internet. It seemed relatively benign. This ten-mile segment was an "up and over" hike. It started on the floor of the irrigated, verdant (thank you, Mr. Mulholland), and highly populated (thank you, incredibly wealthy land developers) Woodland Hills in the San Fernando Valley. The trail then crossed Mulholland Drive, a dirt path at this point, passed over the ridge of the Santa Monica Mountains before descending to the ocean at Pacific Palisades. The route roughly paralleled Topanga Canyon Road, which was slightly to the west, and came as close as possible to the city-limit line, which, remarkably, took a rationally appearing course through the wilderness. (I guess there were no conflicting interests at play to gerrymander the boundary.)

I invited both Thomas and Carl to join me. Carl had recovered from his scrapes and bruises and had replaced his phone but nonetheless demurred. Thomas and I had a great day—redemption after the Castle Peak agony. The wildflowers were everywhere exploding with color, the result of thorough waterings they had received from recent rainfall.

As is common for the mountains near the ocean, especially early in the day, clouds hung low and added a sense of mystery or isolation. A large sandstone outcropping lords over the valley, and with only a touch of imagination, earns its designation—Eagle Rock. Wings spread, it could hop off its perch and float away on the next thermal.

(There is a second Eagle Rock stone formation that I encountered toward the end of my trek. Rather than a rock formation itself, it is the shadow of a soaring bird that the sun casts on the irregular surface of a massive stone dome. It rises out of the wooded foothills in a neighborhood known, of all things, as Eagle Rock.)

The Chumash Indians populated this area perhaps 11,000 years ago and developed one of the most complex non-agricultural societies in the world. The Tongva people arrived about 8000 years later. It is all a state park now, so the area's isolated nature will remain. No traces of either group were evident, but in the 1920s and '30s, land values in this remote and steeply carved area were low, and well-to-do Angelenos established mountain retreats.

We stopped at Trippet Ranch, 82 acres of rugged woodland purchased by Cora Trippet in 1917. This was a weekend retreat, and the family had carved out a large enough flat area to include skeet shooting as one of their activities. Cora's son oversaw the building of a more elaborate ranch house in the 1940s. It is extant and, despite its unlikely and remote location, represents the best work of two architects who pioneered a regional style that blended modern and traditional trends.

On a ridge nearby, with or without low clouds, the best vista was looking down a thousand feet to see Topanga Canyon Road twisting up the gorge. Somewhere nearby on the intervening wooded slope, a resort, Elysian Fields, was in business for the last third of the 20th century. I would be amiss in a chapter about nature to not mention this nudist camp, which in its heyday had over 1000 members. If it hadn't closed because of financial difficulties, I would have had to find my way down to pay a visit. Clothes were optional, hugs were ok, sex wasn't. Newbies often asked where they should point their eyes. "Look wherever you want, just don't stare."

Tom and I exited the wilderness onto Los Liones Drive, walked past a wonderful mural that I will describe later, reached Pacific Coast Highway, summoned an Uber, and called it a day. I had now walked 12 of my anticipated 34 ten-mile segments, six of these were wilderness treks that I have just described. Going forward, there would be just one more walk in the wild, the return to Mt. Lukens' summit several months in the future. In the interim, there were low-altitude natural attractions that caught my attention.

I heard the first ones before I saw them. At a corner market in Chatsworth, I had asked where I could get a bird's eye view of the Chatsworth Reservoir and Preserve where I had recently seen a fenced-off lime kiln. "Cross the street, walk up through the neighborhood. You'll see it all." While ascending the steep residential street, I began to hear loud screeches, and the sources soon revealed themselves—peacocks. They were everywhere, in the street and atop fences, cars, and rooftops. They were indifferent to my interest in photographing them.

According to a driver of a car creeping down the street while waiting for a screeching pair to finish crossing, "They're busy proclaiming their fitness to breed."

"Does their noise bother you?"

"You get used to it."

I'm not sure I could. Back at the corner market, I talked to a local who was a real estate agent. I asked, "When you sell, do you have to disclose that peacocks are part of the deal?"

"Yes, that and mountain lions."

Hmmm… He also told me that the peacocks may have escaped years ago from Roy Rogers' ranch, which was nearby on Trigger Street. (By the way, Dale Court is the next street over. Both streets have signage proclaiming, "Slow. Peacock Crossing.") He said that the free-range screechers are protected. One impatient driver hit and killed one. Fortunately or unfortunately, a security camera captured the event, and the perpetrator paid a $3000 fine and attended an anger management program. Hmmm…

By contrast, trees are not noisy and are less likely to be driven over; and I like them, especially those that are lucky enough not to have any nearby competition or whack-job pruning. These are out in the open and can be appreciated for their form and scale either from a distance or up close, neither of which is possible with just a drive-by. I found my favorites in long-established cemeteries: Wilmington, Oakwood Memorial Park Cemetery in Chatsworth, and Forest Lawn, which is partly in Glendale and partly in LA (I'll explain later). Additional arboreal treasures exist in LA's city parks, especially in Point Fermin and Averill Parks in San Pedro. I would have loved to stop and take a nap under the wonderful trees on the campuses of Occidental College and California State University Los Angeles.

The granddaddy of them all, however, is the 100-foot-tall El Pino Famoso, situated on a vacant residential lot on a hilltop east of downtown LA. By a foot or two, it might be in the unincorporated area of East LA rather than in the incorporated behemoth of Los Angeles. I don't think El Pino cares, and it can be admired from

miles around in every direction, so I am including it. Also, it is not a pine as most people know it, but a bunya pine, which is native to Queensland, Australia. It probably was planted in the 1940s by a Japanese dentist who had been interned during World War II and was given this plot by a woman who worked with his wife.

Even dead trees can be fascinating. I saw charred remains in every one of the six wilderness areas where I hiked. None of the areas looked at all burned out when I passed through, but the relics made me realize that wildfires have long been ubiquitous around LA's borders and that wilderness mends quickly. The Station Fire roared up the slopes of Mt. Lukens in 2009. In 2024, I had to look closely under dense vegetation to see the remnants.

I also like tree stumps and often stopped to study them. "Which ring identifies my birth year?" Which one formed the year LA was founded?" Gradually with weathering, radial cracks appear in the stump, giving it a starburst and cosmic appearance. Way to go, trees.

Next, I took my exploration of natural attractions to an area that begins no more than a foot or two above sea level. This is where Ballona (remember, buy-YO-nah) Creek opens into an estuary, which is now the Ballona Wetlands Ecological Preserve. It measures slightly over a mile square, which makes it the second-largest open space in Los Angeles, topped seven times over by Griffith Park. At one point, Howard Hughes owned much of this area and built a private airport there for his aircraft company. In its hangars the Spruce Goose, the largest airplane ever built up to that time, came to life. Hughes originally planned to float this flying boat across the Ballona wetlands to the ocean and use Santa Monica Bay as a runway. That plan was scrapped, and a house-moving company transferred the monstrous bird in sections to Long Beach. No telling what insult the Spruce Goose might have inflicted on the wetlands.

Hughes did, however, build a mixed-use neighborhood, Playa del Rey, on a filled-in part of the wetland and agreed that the rest would remain untouched. Developers have perennially lusted for those leftovers, but for now, the marsh seems adequately protected, not only from bulldozers but also from mere pedestrians. One can walk around the fenced perimeter and peek in. With binoculars one can witness an amazing array of birdlife.

The Friends of Ballona Wetlands offer monthly guided tours inside the preserve. I joined one and learned that the Tongva Indians held this site sacred, built their thatched huts next to the wetlands, and hunted, fished, and buried their dead there. We walked along a raised area into the middle of the marsh to an observation deck. From there we had prime bird spotting in the foreground and Playa del Rey condos and apartments in the background. Running between nature and civilization was a berm, perhaps 40 feet wide and raised well above the high tide mark. It is a roadbed, a vestige of the Pacific Electric Railway Company, popularly known as the Red Cars, whose lines octopussed the region and enticed visitors to become residents and residents to become homeowners, preferably on property sold by the developer who owned the transit line.

The final noteworthy nature attraction along my route occurs repeatedly and exclusively on the Southern California and Baja California beaches. On the receding high tide, it occurs twice a month under either a new or full moon—sex in the sand. Millions take part in front of curious onlookers. Before your imagination runs wild, the millions are five-to-seven-inch-long sardine-like critters known as grunion. The spectators are human peepers who come to marvel at the spectacle.

From March through August, when the tides are the highest, the female grunions beach themselves, stand on the tails, wiggle themselves halfway into the wet sand, and deposit their eggs. The males then curl around and offer their sperm. The next wave comes in and they all happily swim away, leaving the fertilized eggs to incubate in the warm, moist environment.

The California Department of Fish and Wildlife's website indicates which nights and between what hours the grunion are predicted. (It is always late at night.) During March and July, looky-loos with fishing licenses can pick up 30 of the sex fiends. During the intervening months, the season is closed so that the fish can maintain their numbers. For the rest of the year, their habits are mysteries.

With these facts in mind, I headed for the beach in Venice at about 11:00 PM on a designated night and stood a few inches inland from where the most recent wave had rolled in. The wet sand was glistening in the moonlight, so I would easily be able to see any wiggling fish washing ashore. The scene was pleasant and relaxing—a nice breeze, stars, a full moon rising, lapping surf, and an occasional gull flying by. A scattering of people up and down the beach seemed focused on their own romantic interests rather than the grunions'.

After 45 minutes and no show, I went home. Twice more I tried, but the grunion stood me up every time. I called the Cabrillo Marine Aquarium in San Pedro and asked if grunion sighting was like snipe hunting. The receptionist reassured me otherwise and said that the grunion-viewing events hosted by the aquarium earlier in the season had been successful with most sessions providing sightings ranked 4 or 5 on the Walker Scale. W-4 is when thousands of fish carry on for up to an hour. W-5 is when there are so many fish way up and down the beach for over an hour that it would be impossible not to step on them. I had encountered three W-0 nights. For the time being, I had to satisfy my voyeuristic tendencies by watching the little squirmers on YouTube.

Later I decided to try one more time farther down the coast, this time at a "Meet the Grunion" event hosted by the Cabrillo Marine

Aquarium. I thought a dozen people might show up for the program that started at 9 PM. There were about 800.

At the aquarium we watched an introductory video and then hatched our own grunion embryos. From the sand, the staff had collected fertilized eggs from the run two weeks before and now passed out small jars each containing a dab of sand, which they then covered with seawater. The eggs need agitation in order to hatch. This occurs naturally when the next high tide rolls in. For us, we simulated the surf by shaking our jars for a minute. Magically, the water was then teaming with faintly visible beasties swimming every which way.

About 11:15 PM, spotters began seeing adult grunion beaching themselves and invited all of us to make the five-minute walk to the shore and join them.

The spectacle was on. Each wave brought hundreds of silver squigglers onto the wet sand. Over the next 20 minutes, thousands flopped around, performed their acts of procreation, and disappeared into the dark. It was a W-3 event for the grunion, an amazing display of nature worth four late-night forays to discover.

Apparently, all that the grunions need from humans is for us to leave them alone. In other instances, however, animals seem to benefit from our intervention.

CHAPTER 5

NURTURE

A population of nearly 4 million residents and another 9 million in the surrounding metropolitan area still leaves some room for a remarkable array of "nature" to be treasured. This sharing of space with native plants and animals is facilitated by the presence of a seacoast and two mountain ranges—the San Gabriel mountains along the northern reaches and the Santa Monica mountains right through the middle. Large nature preserves and wilderness parks ranging in elevation from sea level to over 5000 feet high also help preserve the wide diversity of plants and animals that this mild climate can support. Nonetheless, with conflicting demands on space and a growing human population, nature can benefit from a boost. Here I describe enterprises that I encountered along the city limits where caring individuals are making a difference.

In attraction-rich Griffith Park (detailed in Chapter 10) I noticed a small sign indicating Toyon Canyon Landfill Restoration Project. "Restoration" sounded like "nurture," so off I went on a two-mile uphill hike away from the developed areas of the park. This took me past the abandoned zoo into a wilderness of gigantic shrubs and small trees. Finally high up, I could see a flat grass-covered area the size of six city blocks, pipes for venting methane, diversion ditches for rainwater, and two robust men walking quickly toward me.

One, who was middle-aged, wore a large backpack and used a trekking pole. His companion, in his twenties, sported a Red Sox T-shirt and was carrying a two-gallon jug of water in each hand without any apparent distress. I greeted them and asked if they knew where I could go to get the best overview of the landfill, which was sealed in 2008 and was now being monitored for 20 years before being returned to nature or maybe developed into playing fields. The older man pointed to a ridge on the skyline ahead as the best viewpoint and invited me to tag along because they were headed that way. He said that I was safe in case of an accident because they were both emergency medical technicians. I informed them that my orthopedic surgery background added backup.

The older man, Tony, explained that he was mentoring his companion, Daniel, who aspired to become a firefighter.

Tony told me he lived in nearby Silverlake, close enough to the extensive wilderness areas of Griffith Park that coyotes (and a mountain lion for a while) would come into his neighborhood looking for dinner. Four years earlier, Tony had begun to think that the "bunnies and squirrels" in the park were not getting enough to eat and drink, which diminished their numbers and meant that the marauders at the top of the food chain had to go to town for dinner. Tony started bringing sustenance into the woods for the little critters. He said the park rangers had looked askance at these handouts until he explained that doing so meant that the predators could remain well-fed and safe within the park, as would dogs and cats in the adjacent residential area.

We walked upwards on a dirt maintenance road before Tony veered off onto a faint, narrow path that steeply ascended through shrubs and grass. Then descending a short distance, we ducked into a branch-and-vine-covered bower. A hummingbird thrummed around two overhead feeders and flitted off. The two men dropped their cargo and set to work.

Daniel used garden pruners to cut five pounds of carrots into coins and scattered them on the ground. Tony similarly distributed 40 pounds of walnuts, almonds, and unshelled peanuts. He scrubbed four or five water bowls and a plastic baseball helmet clean and filled them with fresh water. The empty hummingbird feeders were replaced with fresh, full ones. He said he made this fully self-financed trip once a week year-round and twice as often in the summer. I asked him if he ever put out a trail cam. He said no. For him, just the satisfaction of seeing the bounty disappear was enough.

Tony snapped open a plastic storage box tucked between gnarled tree roots and produced a guest book, which he invited me to sign. Daniel also signed it since it was his first visit too. Flipping through it, I saw that others had visited the bower. Tony had also recorded his own thoughts and observations, which he was planning to transform into a book.

They packed up, and we waded through the tall grass back to the dirt road. Tony and Daniel continued up to supply a second oasis. I turned the other way and headed down. I had obtained the view I wanted of the landfill restoration project—and much more.

I came across other altruistic Angelenos. Like Tony, they spend a lot of their time helping animals in less remote sites.

Nickie Mingarelli is the founder of Love Always Sanctuary for farm animals. Located in Sunland along the northern boundary of LA, her ranchette is home to rescued pigs, goats, sheep, donkeys, chickens, ducks, geese, and turkeys. It is generally sunny (and hot) in Sunland, so special attention is paid to the sensitive skin of the pigs. One gets a regular slathering of zinc oxide sunblock on its ears, and another one across its back. "He hates it."

Nickie is vegan, and so are her wards, except for one ironic but practical exception. Eggs produced by chickens get tossed on the ground of their roost and are instantly and enthusiastically consumed. The sanctuary backs up to wilderness, so all the enclosures for the birds are covered to prevent nearby hawks and coyotes from indulging in their entirely non-vegan habits. Visits are by reservation, and there is an "open barn" most Saturdays, private tours and petting sessions for groups of up to 12; and remarkably, date nights, which include a gourmet vegan meal prepared by Nickie. If you fall in love with an animal, you can sponsor it for $10 per month, which allows you to receive pictures and text updates.

Whereas Love Always Sanctuary rescues and nurtures farm animals in distress, the Wildlife Learning and Conservation Center, located in the same general area near the northern city border, does so for 100 displaced, rescued, and zoo-born wild animals. Paraphrasing their mission statement, the animals more than earn their keep by aiding public education, inspiring wildlife and environmental protection, and encouraging a deep interest in zoology. It is a small zoo with some special features and creatures. For instance, a bald eagle's permanently injured wing renders it flightless; and Zeus, a Western Screech Owl, is blind. These infirmities don't detract from the birds' beauty and dignity, and they help visitors understand what it means to be both wild and disabled. A rescued boa constrictor was being fed properly so that normal growth, which surprised and then overwhelmed its original owner, was restored. When I visited, it was 16 feet long. The crocodile swimming in the pool was surely happier than it was when confined to a bathtub, as it had been prior to its rescue.

Even though some of the zoo's residents have been restored to health, I was told they would not do well if released into their natural habitats, which in some cases were thousands of miles from LA.

Two special programs at the Wildlife Learning Center extend its outreach. One is to bring observers close to the animals. For a fee beyond the modest general admission charge, a visitor can have an "individual animal experience." Their two-toed sloth, three-banded armadillo, porcupine, and red-tailed boa were among the options.

I chose to meet Ruger, an adolescent giraffe, who was not a zoo resident but rather an across-the-fence neighbor in a horse paddock. When the zookeeper, who was carrying a tub of romaine lettuce, and I approached the fence, Ruger came right over and enthusiastically accepted these offerings from my hand. When he leaned down to receive the lettuce and nose pats, we had a close encounter. I already knew that giraffes have tongues that can wrap around and grasp food to pull it into their mouths, but I had never seen this useful maneuver up close. By standing face-to-face with Ruger, I marveled at how he folded the tip of his tongue sideways to trap the lettuce leaf between the upper surface of the tip and the upper surface of his tongue farther back.

While I was trying, unsuccessfully, to emulate that foraging maneuver, the zookeeper told me that Ruger would soon be moving to his permanent home in Texas because at maturity, he would be too tall for him and his enclosure to fit under bridges along the way. The only alternative that I could imagine was that every time the truck came to an underpass, Ruger would step down and walk under, maybe with the enticement of a basket of romaine.

The Center's other outreach program brings animals close to observers. The array of animals taken to a school for demonstration and discussion could include a porcupine, snake, rabbit, bullfrog, red-tailed hawk, armadillo, and California desert tortoise.

At another facility, people are helping dogs and cats. How unlucky it is for one to be abandoned and sent to a shelter. Yet how lucky if that shelter turns out to be the Wallis Annenberg PetSpace in Playa del Rey. Mrs. Annenberg is well-known

in Southern California for her extensive and visionary philanthropic work. An example is providing funding for a vegetation-enhanced overpass spanning the ten-lane Ventura Freeway. When complete, wildlife, particularly mountain lions who need large territories to survive, can transit safely in their natural habitat without having to dodge speeding cars.

PetSpace is equally innovative and entirely rethinks the dismal image of a stinky, noisy, depressing dog pound. Entry into this modern, glass-walled building leads to a bright soaring atrium and a visitor counter. To the left is a dog grooming school, where the resident canines as well as area pets can come to look their finest. To the right, steps lead up to the kennel area, where dogs and cats all seem so serene in their individual units. Their temporary homes include artificial grass, bedding, toys, and picture windows with ventilated panels through which the animals can view and sniff their prospective owners. There is an adjacent open area where standup comedians perform on Friday evenings with neighborhood dogs and their human families in attendance.

School tours are also a regular part of PetSpace's outreach, as is the fostering program, where big-hearted animal lovers provide temporary care in their homes for special-needs animals. These include newborns that require bottle feeding and older pets recovering from medical treatment or surgery. Summertime brings two week-long day camps. Critter Camp teaches kids about animal health, behavior, care, nutrition, ecology, biology, and adoption. Pet Pioneer Camp infuses information and activities about grooming, exercise, photography, and veterinary medicine into the learning and fun. If you need a boost of feel-good spirit, a visit or contribution to PetSpace will do it.

Another feel-good animal care facility, where barking might be heard but adoption is not an option, is the Marine Mammal Care Center in San Pedro. The day I visited, 29 northern elephant seals, two harbor seals, and 48 California sea lions were in residence, all recovering from illness or injury and consuming 650 pounds of fish a day in the process. The caretakers here take pains to minimize human contact with these wild animals. For instance, they use plywood panels between themselves and their patients to nudge them around for transport to the treatment room and to clean their pools and sun decks. Rescue and rehab, along with education and research, comprise the Center's aim to promote ocean conservation. A video clip streaming in the gift shop highlighted success stories with images of newly discharged patients vigorously bee-lining across the beach, diving into the surf, and returning home.

Turning right out the Marine Mammal Care Center's front door and taking 20 steps across the parking lot brought me to the Oiled Bird Rescue and Education Center. My planning had not identified this as a point of interest, so my curiosity was suddenly piqued. A sign on the door, however, explained that to control their patients' stress, visitors were not allowed. One can, however, glimpse recovery in progress by watching their PeliCam live-stream video, which displays their large outdoor flight aviary.

Tucked just inside the northwest "shoulder" of Los Angeles city limits is Chatsworth, a neighborhood popular with horse lovers. Modern residential developments are slowly encroaching on this semirural area, where one-to-three-acre plots often include paddocks and weathered barns fronted by modern homes.

Halfway up a rough, dead-end gravel road, a small sign read, BEWARE OF GUINEA PIG. I was intrigued and went in for a visit. A larger sign indicated that this was the Los Angeles Guinea Pig Rescue and Adoption Center. It was Saturday afternoon, and 150 adorable, adoptable piggies were on display exuding their charm. Human families, which often included young girls, were bringing their pets back in for quarterly health checks, nail trimming, and ear cleaning. A young couple had brought their Jellybean with them to find an adoptive friend. A staff member directed them to possible same-sex matches, and the couple made a tentative decision. Then Jellybean and her new acquaintance spent ten minutes together in a pen to ensure their compatibility. They nudged each other, shared a lettuce leaf, and showed no signs of aggression or temerity. The new owners showed a picture of their home pen, which needs to be at least two feet by three feet. After confirmation all around and payment of the $45 adoption fee, off they went.

The Center's owner said that at times the census doubles or even triples. In one instance, she rescued 200 to 300 neglected guinea pigs from "up north" that were possibly being raised for snake food. The actual count of refugees from that trip was uncertain because an unidentified number of the sows were pregnant. The Center also boards previously adopted pets for $12.50 a day, so the census climbs markedly around the December holidays.

The piggies are incredibly cute with their large, expressive eyes, faint squeaks, and cuddly nature. Should you be interested, think in terms of multiples since one of these highly social critters by itself will be lonely. (I learned that in Switzerland it is considered inhumane and therefore illegal to have just one guinea pig.) Finally, take a picture of your home pen with you to ensure that it passes muster.

Physically close, the Kindred Spirits Care Farm is 300 hundred yards away at the end of the road where the Guinea Pig Rescue Mission is located. Logistically, however, visiting both venues requires two trips because Kindred Spirits admits visitors only on Sundays whereas the guinea pig haven is open exclusively on Saturdays. It is worth two trips, however, because the piggies are so cute, and at Kindred Spirits, humans help animals *and* vice versa.

Care farms are common in Europe and are catching on in the United States. Twelve are scattered across California. The Care Farming Network defines their purpose as the therapeutic use of farming practices to benefit marginalized or vulnerable individuals. Kindred Spirits takes this mission one step further by making itself a home for abused, neglected, or abandoned farm animals. Each of the one hundred pigs, turkeys, sheep, goats, cows, and alpacas have human names, which engenders a human connection: Charles Bukowski is an alpaca; Tallulah, a pig; and Serafina, a most affectionate sheep. Docents lead visitors through the enclosures, bring them face-to-face with the residents, and recount the animals' histories. For instance, Emma, a turkey, grew up in a factory farm enclosure with little room to move or turn around. Once rescued, she was confused by breezes blowing her feathers and by a bug crawling through the grass under her feet.

She acclimated easily once she gained strength to strut again.

The refugees share their large enclosures with Sunday visitors along with daily volunteers who may have been abused, neglected, or abandoned themselves. Kindred Spirits works closely with John R. Wooden High School, eight miles away, and involves students who are at risk for dropping out. While earning high school credits, the students volunteer at Kindred Spirits and can learn about agriculture, plant and soil science, and behavior and nutrition, both for humans and other animals. Caring for animals that previously experienced starvation, disease, or injury naturally promotes compassion, direction, healing, and hope for at-risk students and adds meaning to their lives. Kindred Spirits also promotes sustainable care farming, which provides knowledge and skills that the students can apply at home and gain satisfaction from watching plants grow. The Care Farm also partners with UCLA professors who are teaching classes titled Food Justice; Civic Engagement; Food: A Lens on Environment and Sustainability; and Philanthropy as Civil Engagement.

Is Kindred Spirits' end-of-the-road location a metaphor for harboring failure? Combined to emphatically imply otherwise are the canopy of old oaks, the spacious, odor-free enclosures, the garden teeming with robust plantings, the knowledge and infectious enthusiasm of the student volunteers, and the friendly animals nudging for one more behind-the-ear scratch.

I have just described my discoveries about ways Angelenos along the city limits are helping animals. I also found sites where animals are helping people.

I discovered Ride On Therapeutic Horsemanship by chance while I was walking along Topanga Canyon Boulevard in Chatsworth between California Firewood Sales (described in Chapter 12) and Valley Hive (described in Chapter 6). Ride On's mission statement includes "... to promote the welfare of at-risk youth and people with any type of physical, intellectual, or cognitive disability by means of equine assisted activities and therapies."

It started humbly in 1994 with volunteers bringing horses from the backyards of three neighbors and providing lessons to a few members of the target clientele. Twenty years later, Ride On was charged with finding 85 horses suitable for 135 athletes with intellectual disabilities to mount for international competitions. Presently it provides over 7000 lessons annually to 250 individuals with disabilities. Services include hippotherapy, which involves physical, occupational, and speech and language therapies that use the horse's movement to facilitate treatment. Apparently, the multidimensional sensory and movement experience improves the client's balance, coordination, strength, speech, and communication. Sunrise Vaulters in Lake View Terrace, also in horse country, takes horsemanship to a higher level. It teaches the art and sport of gymnastics on horseback, i.e., vaulting. The history of vaulting goes back as far as Roman times when acrobats would perform on the backs of cantering steeds. Presently it is not only a form of circus-type entertainment, but also for competition, recreation, and—as at Sunrise Vaulters—therapy.

I found the vaulters at the back of the Monte Verde Ranch Equestrian Center, past the California Polo Club, stables for 150 horses, and multiple arenas. A Percheron horse, with its favored smooth gait and broad back, was slowly walking in a 50-foot diameter circle on a lunge line while a young woman on its back was performing a prescribed series of acrobatic poses in harmony with the horse's movement. Autistic kids and wheelchair-bound individuals benefit from interacting with the horse and a coach and from performing simple moves with the help of spotters.

Never having had a particular affinity for horses, I declined a trial ride and walked down the road to learn an important way that dogs are helping people. By a few days, I had missed the annual open house at Guide Dogs of America | Tender Loving Canines; but when I contacted them and explained my journey, the staff gave me a tour, so I gained a sense of the open house experience.

GDA | TLC is spread out over a peaceful seven-acre campus in a residential neighborhood in Sylmar. Lawns, walkways, and towering pine trees, separate the modern, one-story buildings. The external ambiance only hints at the amazing love and attention contained within. Employees are encouraged to bring their own dogs to work; and for some, that is a practical matter because they are vision impaired as are many of the organizations' clients. GDA | TLC also provides service dogs to veterans with PTSD and to autistic children.

I learned that the matching process begins with a breeding program for Labrador retrievers and sometimes for Labs crossed with golden retrievers. Fur color doesn't matter. Outbreeding, calm temperament, and intelligence do. While pups are still nursing, volunteers provide purposeful play to begin conditioning the dogs to be comfortable and calm even when exposed to unexpected voices, loud noises, and obstacles both underfoot and overhead. Two cats wander the campus and aid the trainees' growing imperturbability. Beginning at this early age, the pups wear shoulder jackets while in training, which remind them that they are working. Working, that is, until the jacket comes off—then it's time to play.

When the pups are eight weeks old, they are farmed out to "puppy raisers," who foster them for 18 months and continue with rudimentary training that includes proper house manners, basic obedience, and

exposure to various community experiences, which allows them to feel safe in all situations.

At any one time, 150 to 200 pups are in foster care. The staff that I spoke with who were also puppy raisers said that their sadness from returning their trainee was balanced by knowing how valuable the dog will be to its new owner. Fosterers often soothe their broken hearts by turning around and fostering again.

When the fostered dogs return to campus, the intense training begins, and it will differ according to whether the pup is going to be a guide dog for a visually impaired or stability-challenged client or a service dog for a veteran or autistic child.

One anecdote told to me was of a Vietnam vet who was experiencing frequent and severe nightmares that caused him extreme panic and agitation. He withdrew to the point that he was not eating, never venturing out, and losing contact with his friends. His daughter suggested to him that he get a service dog, but he declined, saying that there were others who needed these companions more than he did. When his daughter relayed his sentiment to GDA|TLC, the response was, "Wrong. There is a dog suited for you and only for you, it would not be right for anyone else." The vet relented and went through the training. This included partnering with his dog, Triton, in the "squish" maneuver.

Triton learned to sense when a crisis was imminent and lie across his owner's thighs. The vet learned to match his breathing with the slow breathing of the dog and was thereby able to relax and regain composure. The result was that the man's whole life was turned around thanks to Triton. He was once again able to go out and reconnect with friends. And his appetite came back. "Good dog!"

On parting, the staff asked me to stress to readers that when these amazing dogs are in harness, they are working, even if they are sitting or lying down. Any distraction such as speaking to the dog, making a sound to attract its attention, touching it, or feeding it could create a dangerous situation for the dog and its owner. When you meet a dog and handler, speak to the human, not the dog; and if you want to pet the dog, ask first. Everybody benefits.

On the city-limits circuit so far, my visit to GDA | TLC and the bird sit were my most peaceful and idyllic experiences. The next neighborhood I explored, worthy of my first Hot Spot award, was far different.

CHAPTER 6

VENICE

Ah Venice—frenetic, zany, free-range. What a change from the serenity and seclusion of the wilderness trail that had delivered me to the edge of the Pacific Ocean several days before. Fortunately, the transition was gradual, both physically and mentally. It started at the Getty Villa, a repository of treasured Greek and Roman art housed in a recreated seaside villa. After my visit, which I describe in Chapter 13, I walked down the coast, with Venice as my eventual target. A stretch along the shore between Lifeguard Towers 17 and 18, designated Ginger Rogers Beach, has long been a gathering spot for the LBGTQ+ community and now rainbow stripes of paint adorn the towers. It was overcast the day I walked by, and the seagulls, the only beachgoers, seemed indifferent to any gender identity issues.

Next, I turned inland and ambled along the border between Los Angeles on the left and Santa Monica on the right. Closest to the beach on the Santa Monica side the homes sit on a bluff and loom over their backdoor neighbors in LA 110 feet below. Two sets of stairways connect the streets, Adelaide above and Entrada and Ocean Avenue Extension below. Whether or not they bind the communities together, they serve as an improvised outdoor gym for urban exercise enthusiasts.

One set is mostly wooden, consists of 170 steps, and shoots straight up the bluff. The other set has 189 concrete steps and more landings, which stagger sections of the climb alternately to the left or right. Regardless of why the landings and turns were built, they mercifully kept me from standing at the bottom and seeing the complete agony all at once. Stair climbers, almost always with earbuds and trance-like expressions in place, had individual styles: two at a time, fast, slow, sideways, hands held high overhead. Nobody looked askance at my unique form—a trekking pole in each hand going up, poles in one hand and the railing in the other going down.

One woman who looked approachable said she was finishing 20 flights. Considering that a story in an office building is generally 13 to 14 feet high, she had just climbed nearly one and a half Empire State Buildings. My thighs were burning after one trip up each set, so I resumed my usual exercise routine, far more interesting even if not so strenuous, and walked on around the 2.5 by 3-mile rectangular bite that Santa Monica takes out of LA's contour along the coast.

Well, almost a rectangle, because one big corner is nipped off to include all of Brentwood Country Club in LA. Otherwise, imagine the confusion if a golfer teed off in one city and putted the same hole in the other. If he won a bet, which city would deserve a cut of his winnings? Far easier to zig the line and put pressing questions like this to rest.

I walked upcountry to the corner occupied by the Country Club, turned right on 26th Street, and checked the street signs. Yep, the ones on the Santa Monica side were narrow blue rectangles with a yellow stripe at the bottom. The Los Angeles ones were in the familiar dark blue. I was on the line. It was one thing to dodge the line around the golf course, but how about where the boundary originally cut obliquely across six residential lots? Imagine sleeping in the same bed as your spouse but being in a different city. Fortunately in 1964, Santa Monica ceded corners of several of these lots to LA, and LA relinquished wedges on a couple of adjacent lots to Santa Monica. Now each of these properties is entirely in one city or the other. This creates a saw-toothed boundary, and in three instances side-by-side neighbors live in different cities.

A little farther along, Centinela (sen-teh-NIL-ah) Avenue becomes the dividing line between Santa Monica and Los Angeles. This stretch is mostly commercial, and I made stops at an array of attractions, including Los Angeles Fine Arts and Wine Storage, Los Angeles International Fencing Center, Motoring Club, and Riot Games Arena. (I'll describe these attractions in later chapters.) To help your orientation, also nearby and tucked in behind University High School is Kuruvunga Springs, which I described in Chapter 1. These attractions were certainly an interesting and diverse mix but didn't fully prepare me for Venice.

I made another right turn just beyond Santa Monica Airport and returned to the coast where I connected with Tammie and her boyfriend, Michael. I had invited them to be my walking partners that day. I had known Tammie for years from her time as a scrub tech

in the operating room, where before both of us retired, we had worked well together. I had learned she was an avid walker and kayaker. I also knew that from surgeons' guff she had to gracefully endure sometimes, she was not easily intimidated. Michael was an avid runner, well-versed in the layout of Venice, and was enthusiastic about joining us. I would enjoy their company, and I also had an ulterior motive (to be revealed later) for inviting them.

Immediately beyond our meeting point, we confronted a 30-foot-tall ballerina/clown made of steel, aluminum, and fiberglass. Clownerina is fastened to the wall of a four-story building above the entrance to a CVS Pharmacy and stands as sentinel to the LA neighborhood of Venice—a suitable introduction to its quirky, lively atmosphere. (I am not sure of Clownerina's preferred pronouns, so I will avoid them even though it is stylistically awkward to use only the noun. Sorry, but Clownerina has Clownerina's sensitivities.) Clownerina sports a

top hat, a red clown nose, a five-o'clock shadow, breasts tucked into a tutu, white gloves, and ballet slippers. Welcome to Venice.

The area is packed with points of interest that are within easy walking distance of each other, so many that Venice is the worthy winner of my first Hot Spot award. One could easily spend an entire day here within a one-mile circle and be forever awed and sometimes shocked, in a fun way. To begin with, a half block away from Clownerina and standing on end at curbside is the four-story-tall *Giant Binoculars*, a sculpture designed by Claes Oldenburg and Coosie van Bruggen. Passage between the binocular's two telescopes, either by car or on foot, brings one to the entrance of Google's campus in Venice. Noted architect Frank Gehry designed the main building, but it plays second fiddle to the binocs.

Two minutes further along, faded lettering across the front of a shuttered one-story box building announces, "Gold's Gym." Joe Gold opened this facility in 1965 at a time when weightlifting and bodybuilding were cultish countercultural activities. Clearly, that time has passed. A couple of streets over, the present Gold's Gym occupies half the block. About a fourth of that space is an outdoor area packed with weight machines. The rest is a cavernous two-story high gymnasium complete with every exercise appliance imaginable. High on the walls, posters of past bodybuilding champs encourage current exercise enthusiasts, and the day we went the place was teeming with them, most of whom were buff. I felt self-conscious and walked on. On consideration, however, I was likely the only self-conscious person in the entire neighborhood, because Venice is synonymous with self-expression and bohemian spirit. How did that come to be?

Here is some backstory.

Venice started with Abbot Kinney. No, Kinney was not an abbot (although maybe his mother hoped he would become one). Rather, Kinney was a conservationist, entrepreneur, and businessman who arrived in Southern California in 1880 at age 30. He bought a foothill property and planted 6000 citrus trees. He was friends with John Muir, who aided him in establishing a timberland reserve that would become Angeles National Forest in the San Gabriel Mountains immediately north of Los Angeles. Kinney and Theodore Lukens, atop whose namesake mountain I started my trek, were contemporaries and shared interests in wilderness conservation and land development.

Kinney bought and sold other pieces of real estate and caught the development bug. In 1891, he bought a mile and a half of swampy oceanfront property that extended nearly a quarter of a mile inland. His vision was to create a simulation of Venice, Italy. Kinney's Venice of America opened on July 4, 1905. By then, canals had been dredged, a new amusement pier extended into the ocean, and the buildings in the downtown business district all had arched arcades simulating those in St. Mark's Square. Electric trolley cars with regular service from downtown LA and adjacent Santa Monica provided easy access.

It was an immediate hit. Visitors marveled at the resort, which they could tour by gondola or miniature steam train before stepping off to roller skate or dance the night away in the huge auditorium on the pier. They were also enticed to buy canal-front residential lots. Many did and built bungalows. Venice thrived. The waterfront became the

Coney Island of the West. The amusement opportunities boggled the imagination—aquarium, carousel, Ferris wheel, Japanese tea house, a ship-shaped restaurant on the pier. Venice hosted a Gran Prix car race, a bathing beauty competition, and a professional baseball team.

Despite Prohibition, Venice continued to grow in wealth and complexity. Subterranean speakeasies were easily accessible beneath those beautifully arched arcades in the business area. Liquor arrived via tunnels from the waterfront. Life along the beach was raucous.

A few blocks inland, however, those who owned homes or had other real estate interests chafed at all the hoopla and the decrepit state of the streets, water supply, and sewer system. They generally supported the idea of having LA annex Venice. The purveyors of pleasure close to the beach were concerned LA would curtail their activities and opposed the idea. At first the petition failed, but two years later it passed. Venice became part of Los Angeles in 1926.

Beachfront Venice proved to be incompatible with automobiles, which contributed to its demise. Kinney had made the area pedestrian friendly with narrow streets. Visitors from afar could easily access the attractions by trolley, but those with cars started amusing themselves elsewhere. Perhaps to ease traffic, but foremost to deal with the problem of stagnant water in the canals, LA filled Kinney's canals in and paved them over. The city leaders downtown otherwise neglected the area to the point that it became known as the "Slum by the Sea." Real estate values plummeted. Low rents attracted bohemian types—artists, poets, musicians--the Beat Generation. In the 1960s, the Hippies took over.

By the early 1970s, Los Angeles recognized the importance of maintaining Venice's character, not so much to attract tourists again but rather to provide housing for low-income individuals. I guess the city leaders were feeling kindly toward Venice because, for a while, nude sunbathing was permissible. Regardless of whether it was sanctioned or not, mural art sprung up on the walls of otherwise nondescript low-rise buildings left over from boom times.

Perhaps coincidentally, an 18-mile bike path that ran from well north of Venice to far south of it was built, and cyclists from those more affluent areas reacquainted themselves with the area as they rode past. Outdoor skating, however, was limited because of the skates' unforgiving steel wheels and the need to wear leather shoes with hard soles on which to clamp the devices. (Remember skate keys?) The introduction of urethane skate wheels in the 1970s changed everything. They were durable, relatively quiet, and gripped the pavement well. Skating and skateboarding blossomed, nowhere more so than on Venice's Ocean Front Walk and the adjacent bike path. Venice became the "Roller Skating Capital of the World."

Currently vendors tout souvenirs, sunglasses, bikinis, tattoos, jewelry, fast food, and novelty art from blankets on the sand or from beachside cubicles. Street performers astounded the vast number of tourists. (Remember the chainsaw juggler?) The funky, eclectic, free-spirited nature of Venice was back and remains so. I am not sure I would want to live there, but it is a blast to visit. A lot of people agree. Venice's 10 million visitors a year make it the second-most visited tourist destination in Southern California. Thank you, Abbot.

After staring at the map of Venice on which I had marked multiple closely spaced points of interest, I realized that there was no way to connect the dots and visit them in any logical order. And to try to do so would be counter to the spirit of Venice, because I do not think that "efficiency" and "Venice" should ever reside in the same sentence. The first time through on my trek, I had my daypack and trekking poles, which made me stand out and attract a little attention in other neighborhoods. But such was not the case on the Venice boardwalk. Nobody turned an eye. They were more likely watching the balding, deeply tanned, overweight character I call Horn Man. I first saw him lounging aimlessly midmorning on a mound of sand beside the bike path. He had a detached air of homelessness and perhaps addiction about him. With a nod, I passed by on my way to Muscle Beach Venice to meet my trainer.

The original Muscle Beach was a mile up the coast in Santa Monica and was the birthplace of the physical fitness boom. During the Depression, the Works Progress Administration installed a platform on the beach, which provided a venue for gymnastic and acrobatic exhibitions. The addition of weightlifting equipment attracted bodybuilders such as Joe Gold, Vic Tanny, and Jack LaLanne. Today that area serves gymnasts and acrobats, while the weightlifting and bodybuilding aspects have moved to the Weight Pen on the Venice Boardwalk. A low fence surrounds an open-air area with weight machines spread around and connects to an adjacent garage-type building shaped like a dumbbell, which houses … dumbbells. A day pass cost $10 for me and $5 for my trainer, Alex, under whose watchful eye I had been lifting weights for several years.

As an enrichment to my trek, Alex agreed to meet me one morning at the Pen to supervise my workout. We started in the "garage" with dumbbells. The big ones had numbers like 90 and 100 molded into them. I guess that they were just for show, because despite my best effort to lift one of them, it remained firmly seated in the rack. Then we went outside, and Alex showed me the ropes on the machines. I looked around. Nobody was along the rail taking photos of me, maybe

because I still had my shirt on; but even more surprising was that two stations down, Horn Man was holding a big weight behind his head and doing sit-ups. Hmmm…

Alex and I finished and walked around the outside of the Pen, where a long row of bronze plaques commemorates honorees in the Muscle Beach Venice Hall of Fame. Alex knew them all. I recognized Joe Gold and Steve Reeves. Because Alex had other clients to train, he left.

I wandered over to the skatepark, which two boarders proudly claimed was world-class. One mentioned that the park was so popular that the only way that officials were able to shut it down during COVID-19 lockdown was to fill the bowls with sand. A scattering of observers stood just outside the rail and stood agape, like me, at the athleticism on display by boarders confident enough to flaunt their skills without helmets or knee pads. Most impressive were two young women in bikinis zooming around the sculpted bowls on inline skates.

Although I generally tried to participate in the various recreational activities that I encountered on my trek, I decided against borrowing a skateboard and taking a run, especially with international tourists looking on. Neither did I feel like I had time to try basketball, handball, or beach volleyball, facilities for which are right there on the beach along with weightlifting and skateboarding.

By this time, it was late morning and artists, jewelry makers, cartoon portraitists, and vendors were setting up their shade canopies and arranging their wares. Who should I encounter? Horn Man. He had claimed his sidewalk-adjacent retail space for the rest of the day and was polishing a lamp base consisting of amorphous lumps of glass wrapped with heavy copper wire. "Hey, I saw you in the Pen earlier. I noticed your devil horns." (At four inches long, black, and adhering to his scalp without the aid of any straps, they were hard to miss.) "Yep, I wear them almost every day. But I have to take them off at night, otherwise my cat eats them while I'm sleeping."

Ah, Venice.

Before turning inland and savoring the quieter parts of Venice, I was confronted by a straight row of eight leaf rakes placed handle-first in the sand at ten-foot intervals with their business ends sticking up. Not far away was an area demarcated by sections of three-foot-high ornamental iron fencing. Contained within were two rows of three-inch-long toy cars lined up in the sand. I'm guessing that there were 30 to 40 cars in each row. The artist of these two installations was standing

nearby. "Are these Matchbox Cars?" "No, I got them at the Dollar Store." "What's the point of the rakes?" "I just think they look nice." He said that he lived nearby, loved the beach, and came out nearly daily to make an artistic statement or two, just because he can. Ah, Venice.

Venice is not entirely weird. Part of the canal system remains and is located three blocks inland from "Idiosyncrasy Central." A trio of developers, contemporaries, and competitors of Kinney dredged four canals in one direction that intersect with two in the other. The canals are protected on the National Register of Historic Places. The homes, separated from the canals by narrow sidewalks, are not. Scattered among the original bungalows are modern, hulking two-story glass-cased boxes. Front yards are shallow but often include interesting, if not funky, kitschy landscaping. Yes, several garden gnomes inhabit the area. Canalside, little pontoon boats, some complete with barbeque grills, were afloat, ready for a party. I was told that outsiders can bring their own non-motorized vessels for a serene water-level tour of the neighborhood. Overall, my stroll in the canal district was better than Valium as a cure for beachfront frenzy.

On scrutiny, other remnants of times gone by are visible. In the business area, several buildings with their stately arched arcades remain, and giant wall murals farther on extend the fantasy. After the Grand Canal was filled in, and once paved over, it morphed into Grand Boulevard. At the traffic circle where Grand Boulevard connects with Windward Avenue and Main Street, a blue gondola rests, reminiscent of the roughly three dozen that came from Italy complete with gondoliers in Venice's heyday.

Abbot Kinney Boulevard is home to trendy one-off shops, upscale restaurants, and art galleries. It runs diagonally through Venice for about a mile. I found it interesting that Kinney has a street named after him, and still-existing canals are named for two of the investors and architects who developed them—Howland and Sherman. Poor Clark, the third member of that team, lost out.

I am not much of a shopper so even posted bargains on sidewalk sandwich boards along AKB did not intrigue me. It was the same for Tammie and Michael, so we quickly breezed up one side of AKB and down the other. Even if AKB seems swanky, its origin near Ocean Front Walk provides some amusing unpredictability.

For instance, about halfway along AKB, a pickup truck was nosed into an alley with its tail flush with the sidewalk. Its driver, sitting on top of the cab with his guitar, microphone, and speaker, was serenading passersby. Steps away, a sandwich board in bright colors proclaimed, If love was blind, you wouldn't need us. Welcome. Designs ready to tattoo on you. I always tried to get actively involved in the points of interest I came across, like tasting reclaimed sewage water and pumping iron at Muscle Beach, so I considered getting a tattoo attesting my love for Venice, my bronze-medal Hot Spot winner, but then I realized that the silver and gold winners down the road would want me to sport tats of them too, so I walked on.

After I thought I had experienced all the attractions in Venice, I came across another "by the way"—a point of interest that my research had not unearthed. Only several times on my 342-mile trek was I emotionally touched by an encounter. The first time was at Campo Cahuenga. Now, by surprise, I was again.

On the northwest corner of Venice and Lincoln Boulevards stands a ten-foot-tall obelisk of polished black marble. It memorializes an event that occurred there in April 1942. With only a couple of days to dispose of their property, over a thousand Japanese Americans reported to this corner to board buses that would take them to Manzanar, a concentration camp far away from the coast. Having brought with them only what they could carry, they were confined there for more than three years. The inscription on the monument sums up the situation perfectly.

MAY THIS VENICE JAPANESE AMERICAN MEMORIAL MONUMENT REMIND US TO BE FOREVER VIGILANT ABOUT DEFENDING OUR CONSTITUTIONAL RIGHTS.

THE POWERS OF GOVERNMENT MUST NEVER AGAIN PERPETRATE AN INJUSTICE AGAINST ANY GROUP BASED SOLELY ON ETHNICITY, GENDER, SEXUAL ORIENTATION, RACE, OR RELIGION.

On the opposite side of the obelisk, several personal observations are inscribed. This one was by Arnold Tadao Maeda. "Instead of being worried about where we were going. I was obsessed with the fact that I had parted with my constant companion, my pet dog, Boy. For a 15-year-old, that was unforgettably traumatic."

Venice resident Mae Kakehashi wrote, "When the camp closed, we were given $25 and told to leave. We had nothing when we left camp—no homes, no jobs, no prospects. It was very hard on all of us."

Getty Villa anchored one end of this "coastal" part of my trek, Venice Beach the other. The contrast between a vast collection of Western civilization's most treasured antiquities at the Getty and the ephemeral trivialities of fake tattoos obtainable along Ocean Front Walk could not be greater. Additionally, consider the constitutional questions raised by the imprisonment of Japanese Americans without the slightest nod to due process. Los Angeles is complex.

Through our day in Venice, Tammie's and Michael's energy and enthusiasm for urban adventuring only grew. They proved to be good company, so before we parted I revealed an ulterior motive for inviting them. "How do you feel about joining me on some other days when the attractions might not be so interesting and the neighborhoods, at least by traditional opinion, might be a bit 'sketchy'? It might be good for me to have walking companions." Immediately they said, "Count us in!"

CHAPTER 7

FLIGHT

When I maximally enlarged the LA city limits map on my computer screen, I identified a potential point of interest named the Sylmar Hang Gliding Association. It was marked north of the appropriately named Foothill Boulevard, just where a new residential area gives way to wilderness—a long, steep slope of chaparral that shoots up to a ridge line 2,200 feet above. In the rainy season, it is here that water-soaked clouds get snagged on this barrier to their usual northern progress and dump prodigious quantities of water before scraping themselves over the ridge and continuing on their way. The water they discharge then begins its way south. Hence, the adjacent "wash" runs perpendicular to the ridge and eventually passes under Foothill Boulevard and farther on into the LA River.

That day, the wash was a quarter-mile-wide, rock-strewn, dry gulch. During a rain it becomes a rage of water and debris racing to the ocean.

This slope also creates seasonal and predictable updraft necessary for hang gliding. From SHGA's "headquarters" marked on the map, a van with pilots and folded gliders takes a 45-minute circuitous route to the ridge and the stepping off point. Then pilots can ride the thermals for hours if they wish, sometimes sharing the thrill with California condors before landing at headquarters. (The condors are on their own for landing sites.) Headquarters consists of a grassy landing strip the size of two football fields placed end to end, a trailer for the

81

on-site resident-member-attendant, and two low buildings that serve as clubhouse and storage facilities.

I wandered by on a Sunday afternoon in January and was offered a lawn chair facing the mountain and shaded by the clubhouse. Six or eight good ole boys, ranging in age from 50 to 70, and several dogs, all younger, were enjoying each other's company. Some were half-watching a football game on a small TV. I scrutinized the sky for airborne club members and saw none. I asked why.

"The wind is from the wrong direction this time of year. The best month is May. You're welcome to come back then. In the meantime, if you want to try it yourself, Andy over there, gives lessons at Dockweiler Beach, just west of LAX. There is a steady, onshore breeze there nearly year-round. The airplanes like it because it reduces the ground speed they need to take off. Beginning hang gliding students can face into the wind, safely run off the top of the sand dune and land close to the water. After gaining competence there, you can come here and jump off the ridge with us."

Without much prodding, I discovered that these not particularly athletic- or adventuresome-looking men were giants among the sport's pioneers. In their time they achieved many "firsts" such as highest altitude (16,000 feet), longest duration (eight hours), and farthest distance (125 miles to Palm Springs). I asked one, "Do you consider yourself a daredevil?" "Oh no. I bungee jumped once and asked myself, 'Why am I doing this?' Never again."

I returned to the club headquarters in May. Pretty much the same group of men welcomed me back, and the same dogs tried to bark me away. I looked toward the ridge and asked, "Why isn't anybody flying?" The wind is too strong and gusty. A group is up there. They'll take off in a little while when the sun is lower and the wind steadies. If you look closely in that saddle just to the right of the highest point on the ridge, you can see the van."

I spotted a white speck and was invited to look through their telescope, which was permanently fixed to a metal picnic table and focused on the launch site. There I could see a gossamer aircraft much wider than the van was long. After a while I heard, "One is up." A spectator described the first one to take off as the "wind dummy," who would be carefully watched by those soon to be airborne, including the wife of one of the spectators. They would be watching the first to launch to see how the wind was blowing.

Conditions proved favorable, and in the next five minutes the others launched and floated above the ridge. I would have liked to see them land, but I had an appointment to keep, so my parting words were, "Hey Andy, I'll see you at Dockweiler."

A month later I met Bob, one of Andy's instructors, at the top of the sand dune and signed without reading the disclaimers, releases, and caveats. I wondered if the verbiage was identical to what I signed to race go carts, fence, box, or escape from psychopathic killers. It would certainly be efficient to have a universal waiver that would also cover consent for surgical procedures.

"Three rules: Keep your eyes on the target, light touch, and stand up straight." Probably good advice for many situations in life. Specifically for that day, they were Bob's final words before he ran down the steeply sloped sand dune beside me while I soared like a bird. Well, at least like a bird gliding toward the surf and just three feet above the beach.

Overhead a gigantic triangular sail supported horizontally on thin aluminum struts kept me airborne for perhaps twelve seconds (the same as Orville's and Wilbur's first flight). Should I want to become a competent hang glider pilot, Bob said that most learners needed 20 to 70 more flights spaced over three to ten days there at Dockweiler Beach to "get the hang of it."

Formerly known as Moonshine Beach, in 1955 the beach was renamed in honor of Isidore B. Dockweiler, a prominent Southern California lawyer and civic leader. (Nothing is known, however, about his interest in hang gliding). The broad beach, backed by 30-foot-high dunes, is perfect for learners because of its steady, nonturbulent onshore breeze and its soft, sandy crash-landing surface. On my second flight I soared to an elevation of five feet for maybe 15 seconds. It was fun, but I reminded myself that I generally preferred outdoor activities that did not require helmets, so I told Bob that I had miles left to cover on foot and more gliding would have to wait.

Just across the road and running parallel with the shore, a chain-link fence topped with four strands of barbed wire encloses several hundred acres of dunes. This area is also devoted to flight, but here it's for the endangered El Segundo blue butterfly, among the first insects to be so listed. The creature is less than an inch across and has bright blue wings when seen from above. For its entire life cycle, the butterfly depends on seacliff buckwheat, which thrives only on a short stretch of unstable sand dunes along the Southern California coast. Adult blues emerge in synchrony with the buckwheat's bloom and spend their life, measured in days, savoring their nectar and demonstrating their superiority over hang gliders by mating and laying eggs. The eggs hatch within a week, and the caterpillars then feed for a month on the buckwheat's flowers and seeds, after which each one converts to an inactive chrysalis and awaits the next summer to start the cycle again.

Unfortunately, oil refining and urban development have threatened the butterfly's unique, seacoast habitat. It seems ironic that a major supporter of the blues and their habitat is the behemoth and adjacent Los Angeles International Airport, whose runways, if extended westward a short distance, would demolish the habitat. Los Angeles, which owns LAX, and the next business down the beach, a Chevron oil refinery, are aiding the removal of exotic plants that compete with the buckwheat.

Fortunately, the butterflies are making a comeback. There were no blues flitting about the day I walked by, but it was nice to know that people are giving these fragile beauties a chance.

It is hard to hold a conversation at Dockweiler Beach or near the butterfly reserve because of planes growling and whining as they lift off almost overhead from LAX. (Apparently the din does not bother the butterflies.) The four runways, each as long as two-and-a-half miles, are oriented east-west and handle one takeoff on average every 90 seconds around the clock. To diminish the ire of residents living just east of the airport, takeoffs all head westward over the beach and ocean unless the prevailing onshore breeze shifts to a pernicious offshore wind. The Los Angeles city limit skirts the south side of the runways; and hugging the city line there, the Flight Path Museum is logically located and appropriately named.

From the first, Southern California was highly attractive to the aviation industry because of its mild climate, abundant open land suitable for airports and airplane assembly, and available labor pool as the area's population exploded. On the museum grounds, there is a marker that commemorates the beginning of over-the-pole flights from Los Angeles to Europe in 1954. Inside the building, visitors can view landings and takeoffs through large picture windows with the associated howl mercifully reduced to a hum.

The museum highlights the airport's history, which began as a dirt landing strip in a barley field used by aviation pioneers in the early 1920s. The area was known as Mines Field, named after the real estate agent who brokered the land deal to develop the area as a bona fide airport. Then in 1928, three 7000-foot runways were built in just under two months in preparation for the National Air Races. This extravaganza drew large numbers of participants and spectators to events that included transcontinental and various shorter races, formation flying, parachute jumping, band concerts, airborne fireworks shows, and model airplane competitions. Two hundred exhibitors touted their wares and services. By arrangement, the site was turned over to the City of Los Angeles at the end of the show to be expanded into a municipal airport. Mines Field became Los Angeles Municipal Airport.

Then in the early days of World War II, the airport and the nearby airplane assembly plants disappeared. At least it looked that way from above 10,000 feet. Because of fears of Japanese air raids on vital infrastructure on the West Coast, Hollywood set designers and artists cooperated with the Army Corps of Engineers to make runways, hangers, and aircraft factories look like ordinary residential or rural landscapes. This entailed spreading gigantic rolls of netting over entire buildings. Fake houses, trees, and streets topped the netting. Runways were painted green. Area workers would even stroll the sidewalks and move their cars from every day to enhance the subterfuge. The threat never materialized.

Because of Burbank Airport's robust competition for commercial flights, the LA Municipal Airport was used only by private pilots and training schools until after World War II, when the facility, now named Los Angeles International Airport, finally enticed Trans World, American, United, Southwest, Western, and Pan American Airlines to begin service there. The Flight Path Museum reflects this aspect of commercial aviation history by displaying airline-specific memorabilia including swizzle sticks, lapel pins, and—believe it or not—paper tickets. Mannequins dressed as flight attendants, complete with their distinctive pillboxes and other head adornments, add to the nostalgia.

I chatted with Daniel, a volunteer docent, and told him that the next stop on my trek was the Proud Bird. His eyes widened as he glanced at his watch. "The Emirates A-380 is going to take off in an hour. The Proud Bird is the best place to watch it." I vaguely recalled that this Airbus creation was the largest passenger airliner ever built and the only one with a full-length upper deck. Daniel, obviously an aviation addict and avid plane spotter, treated a potential sighting of the A-380 like others might value meeting a rock star. I nodded in appreciation for the tip, recovered my walking sticks from the front desk, and headed for the Proud Bird.

Previously a full-service restaurant, these days an upscale food court and events venue, the Proud Bird abuts LAX on its eastern end. On display in the parking lot and out back in a large open area is a score of full-scale replica vintage aircraft, mostly fighter planes, many mounted on pedestals to recreate a sense of flight—a plane on a stick. These include the P-80 Shooting Star, America's first fighter jet, which saw action during the Korean War, and the Bell X-1, a.k.a. Glamorous Glennis, which powered Chuck Yeager to Mach 1.07 in 1947 when he piloted the first flight to break the sound barrier.

(Because of this event's military significance, it was not made public for another eight months.)

The area out back also includes a comfortable seating area, which as Daniel said, is a perfect site from which to watch planes, especially for landing, not so much for watching them take off. At the predicted time, the Emirates flight taxied, turned, and took off unceremoniously, mostly concealed from the Proud Bird by a tall blast deflector that allows cars on the adjacent Aviation Boulevard to remain upright. The only way I knew it was the A-380 was that the top third of the fuselage was visible above the deflector, compared to only the tail sections of lesser craft.

To commemorate the aviation pioneers who helped boost Los Angeles into its preeminent position, the Flight Path Museum has imbedded bronze plaques along a four-block stretch of sidewalk on both sides of Sepulveda Boulevard just north of LAX. Honorees include some who may not be household names but whose contributions can be easily surmised: Alan Lockheed, Glenn Martin, John Northrop, and Donald Douglas, for instance. Others are well-known: Orville and Wilbur Wright, Chuck Yeager, Amelia Earhart, Charles Lindbergh, and Rosie the Riveter. Without the Walk of Fame, the contributions of others, especially women, might get lost forever: Bessie Coleman, the first licensed black pilot, man or woman; Katherine Cheung, the first Chinese American licensed pilot as well as a lecturer on aviation safety; and Jacqueline Cochrane, the founder of Women's Airforce Service

Pilots and the first woman to pilot a jet. The presence of Starbucks outlets on both sides of the street along the Walk offers an enhanced degree of amiability to the learning experience.

Much later in my counterclockwise trek around LA and almost directly across town from the cluster of flight-related points of interest

 near LAX, I visited the Portal of the Folded Wings Shrine to Aviation in Valhalla Memorial Park Cemetery, which is sprawling and as flat as a marble slab. The site is as near Hollywood Burbank Airport as the Proud Bird is to LAX—just across the street and just as important. The 75-foot-tall shrine, officially described as Mission Revival style, looks to me like an ornamented, half-sized Arc de Triomphe topped with a mosaic-clad dome. It was built in 1924 as a grand entrance to the Memorial Park. Over ensuing years, the din from the increasingly busy airport caused the owners to shift the entrance to the other side of the cemetery, a 15-minute walk, which left the shrine out in left field. That is, until aviation history activists took note.

As the airplane industry had clustered and exploded in the vicinity of LAX, so it also did around the Hollywood Burbank Airport. One avid enthusiast worked for over two decades to have the shrine repurposed to honor pilots, mechanics, and other pioneers of flight. So now it is a mausoleum for the cremated remains of 15 buried there and plaques remembering the contributions of others interred elsewhere—"The Honored Dead of Aviation." They include the inventors of the compound folded wing, useful for packing planes together on aircraft carriers and of the first aerobatic plane. Theirs are not household names, but their intrepid endeavors live on.

For instance, John Moisant designed and built the first all-metal plane. That was 1909. Maybe he should have stopped there. But no, the next year he was the first to fly a passenger across the English Channel. It was Moisant's sixth flight overall and his cat's first. Later that year Moisant raced a Packard car five miles and lost. The following day he fell out of his plane in turbulent conditions and died.

Another extreme adventurist was Hilder Florentina Smith, an aerial acrobat and parachutist. Her dance with death came during her second jump when the chute lines tangled. She cleared them just in time to have the chute open, but it was clear that she, a non-swimmer, was going to land in the ocean. With her husband, the pilot, looking on, she finally drifted inland and landed on the beach. This event inspired her husband to invent and patent the first modern parachute. I am not sure she tested his prototypes. She lived to be 87.

Another pilot recognized at the Portal of Folded Wings defied death. Beyond imagination, Dale Black crashed into the Portal on takeoff from Hollywood Burbank Airport. He was badly injured but lived and then dedicated the remainder of his career to God and aviation safety.

Fairly early on my trek, I witnessed a plane coming apart in midair and splintering beyond repair on impact. Fortunately, the pilot only suffered a damaged ego because he was on terra firma the whole time. This was at Our Model Aviation Club in Sylmar, which is in the far northwest corner of the LA city limits with the base of serious-looking mountains looming to the north. The members lease the riverbed space for their 400-foot runway, shade pavilion, and parking lot from the Army Corps of Engineers, which tries to channel stormwater gushing off the mountains and knows that any structure in this area will eventually be washed into the ocean.

I came across the club purely by happenstance, which was a great recurring pleasure of my trek—discovery! This "by the way" came while I was on my way to the Sylmar Hang Gliding Association's landing site. Walking north toward the mountains, a newish residential area on the left had a few vacant lots remaining. On the right, the land dropped away quickly to the brush-spattered wash. It was about half a mile across and far enough down that at first I didn't see the club facilities. On a closer look, the flat, straight runway stood out among the boulders strewn about by the last torrent. I asked myself, "What's down there?" I squinted and saw a windsock. "I've gotta have a look."

So I backtracked a half mile to access a gravel road that gently transited from street to club level along the side of the wash. As I approached, I could see a model plane doing aerobatics, but it was strange because I didn't hear its engine. Five or six pilots were sitting in lawn chairs watching the show. Others were sitting in the shade at a picnic table with their toolboxes open and their planes opened up. They welcomed me and my questions, which started with, "Does anybody still use piston engines, or all your motors electric?" "Electric. The battery and motor are much lighter than the old piston engines, fuel tanks, and fuel." Another pilot added, "The battery gives about ten minutes of flying time, and there is a clock on my controller. Even if the engine dies, there is enough juice in the battery for me to glide the plane into a safe landing."

I knew from limited experience trying to fly a drone and a radio-controlled glider that controlling the craft is tricky when it is flying toward you because the craft's "left" is my "right" and vice versa. In other words, if I want to send the craft to my right, I have to push the joystick to the left. The classic way to learn this counterintuitive maneuver is to turn your back to your baby and watch it over your shoulder. Then right is right and left is left. The group agreed that trying to control the plane when it was flying upside down added another level of complexity. One pointed out that an onboard camera can provide a cockpit view, which the pilot watches with video goggles. I asked, "How long does it take to have full mastery of the controls?" "For most pilots, two to three planes." Equally deadpan, "We are pilots. Pile it here. Pile it there."

The plane that I saw crumble itself into a pile had lost a wing flap, making it uncontrollable. Several of us walked through scrub brush to the crash site and helped the pilot pick up the pieces. It was interesting to see the carefully crafted, light-weight interior support structures and control cables, now all in a snarl. Acknowledging that it was beyond  repair, the pilot didn't seem distressed, more resigned. I quietly asked somebody else. The answer was $350.

Another hobby involving flight has considerable startup costs, but in time it can turn a profit in addition to just providing fun and teaching something about animal behavior. To learn about beekeeping, I took a two-hour class at The Valley Hive, which is in Chatsworth, about a 10-mile walk from the hang gliding and model aircraft clubs in the northern part of the San Fernando Valley. The business was another of those wonderful things I never knew existed until I walked past the building and saw the sign. It is mostly a nursery but also a haven for beekeepers, beekeeper wannabes, and bees. Their shop sells the equipment, supplies, and bees as well as the end product. They also have introductory classes and a six-week course. On the day I happened by, I both signed up for the next introductory class and bought a pound of Avocado Honey. (I had to ask. It's the avocado flower, not the fruit, that flavors this variety of honey.)

On a Sunday morning several months later, about 30 people were in attendance for our introductory class. Keith Roberts, co-owner of The Valley Hive, first told us about the history of beekeeping (it goes back at least 10,000 years), then about the rudiments of bee anatomy and behavior, hive structure, and various bee enemies, including pesticides, pests, pollution, and diseases. Home beekeeping is legal in Los Angeles with a limit of one hive per 2500 square feet of lot area. That means that even small residential lots can have two hives. Female worker bees, once laden with pollen collected as far as five miles from home, make a beeline for the hive. This makes for an interesting element of the city ordinance, Hobbyist hives have to be a minimum of five feet from the property line and with a wall/fence/hedge at least six feet high separating the hive from the adjacent property or have each hive at least eight feet off the ground. This way, interaction between the bees and "individuals in the vicinity" will be minimized.

A colony has about 60,000 bees, and it takes 2 million flower visits by the female worker bees to make a pound of honey and nine times that many visits to make a pound of waxy comb. Through a glass wall in the shop, we observed a hive in full action. The beekeeper had marked

 the queen with a green dot, so she was easy to spot as she laid fertile eggs that would develop into female worker bees and unfertile ones that would become male drones.

Then we suited up and headed for the apiary where we learned about hive maintenance and watched Keith harvest several combs that the bees had completely filled with honey and sealed off. Back in the shop, he sliced off the wax layer covering the comb with a hot knife and then put the combs in a spinner to sling the honey out. We each received a small jar of the freshly harvested honey to take home.

He said that it might take $1000 to get started with hives, protective equipment, smoker, spinner, and starter bees, including a queen. Keith stressed that the queens The Valley Hive sold were all from Northern California and were docile European honeybees. Aggressive, Africanized, ones have been slowly working their way north and provoking anxiety after escaping in 1957 from a lab in Brazil, but it is too cold in Northern California for these terrorist bees to survive there.

Keith noted that since honey does not support microorganisms or toxins regardless of time or temperature, it is legal for apiarists to sell it at farmers' markets and other informal venues. Although the initial investment is sizable, the ongoing care is minimal, and a hive can produce 60-100 pounds of honey a year. Do the math. A pound of honey in The Valley Hive shop costs $14.95.

On small paper spoons, I sampled four varieties defined by what the nearest flowering plant to the hive was when the honey was produced. Sage was the lightest, not particularly flavorful to my taste. Citrus was sweeter. The shopkeeper described the buckwheat as savory and lingering. By this time, I began wondering if there was a snobbery in honey tasting akin to wine tasting. Buttery? Bright? Complex? Delicate? Spicy? Earthy? With that preoccupation, I forgot what the buckwheat tasted like, but I did like the avocado—it was molasses-like.

At the end, Keith made a brief and impassioned point. Consider that honeybees, except for the queen, live for only four to six weeks. They cannot survive in solitude but rather spend their short lives in close quarters and in harmony with tens of thousands of their genetically identical siblings. They depend on one another to provide special functions for the sake of the colony. Hmmm... Now every time I see a honeybee, I wonder if it is modeling behavior that might benefit any other species.

CHAPTER 8

REFLECTION

Isaac Newton Van Nuys' mother apparently aspired for her son to become a physicist, astronomer, and mathematician like his namesake, but she was probably proud of the way he turned out anyway. He was the second of seven children and the only one named after a famous person.

Isaac moved to California from New York in 1855, five years after California achieved statehood. He must have done well as a country-store owner in Northern California, because within 16 years he had moved south and bought into Isaac Lankershim's San Fernando Homestead Association, which owned nearly the south half of the San Fernando Valley—60,000 acres, nearly 100 square miles. (He also married Lankershim's daughter.) The Homestead Association transitioned from farming sheep to growing dryland wheat, and in 1876 the Association filled two grain cargo ships at the LA Harbor in San Pedro with Valley grain. It was the first California grain shipped from Los Angeles.

The Association sold out to the Los Angeles Suburban Homes Company in 1911, whose directors wanted Los Angeles to annex the holding. Then they could share the upcoming massive influx of water channeled south from the Owens Valley and develop this former and parched rancho into residential areas and intensely farmed orchards.

Van Nuys died in 1912, and the aqueduct began irrigating the San Fernando Valley a year later. Three years after that, Los Angeles brought this vast expanse of land under its jurisdiction by annexing it and agreeing to dispense water and public services in return for an increased number of taxpayers.

In due time, streets were named within the property that they once owned to memorialize both the Lankershim family and Van Nuys. (Shouldn't we all be so lucky.) Van Nuys Boulevard runs north-south through the heart of the San Fernando Valley and the neighborhood that straddles it is known by the same name.

Isaac Lankershim got only a street. It runs obliquely for about seven miles through the North Hollywood neighborhood of Los Angeles and partly covers the foundation stones of Campo de Cahuenga. Recall that it was there that Lieutenant Colonel John C. Frémont and General Andrés Pico signed a seminal treaty between the US and Mexico (see Chapter 1).

Only a short street in downtown LA memorializes Frémont.

Conversely, Pico, who represented the losing side in that massive land transfer, had a 15-mile boulevard running from downtown LA to the beach named for him, maybe out of gringo gratitude. If not for the transfer, LA might still be part of Mexico.

An Irish immigrant named Andrew Boyle also did well in the namesake sweepstakes. He bought 22 acres of land east of downtown LA on a bluff overlooking the LA River in 1858 and later expanded his holdings. Four years after his death in 1871, his son-in-law subdivided the property for residential development and named the area in Boyle's memory. Shouldn't all sons-in-law be so thoughtful?

For reasons I do not understand, Van Nuys, his wife, and his in-laws—i.e., her parents, the Lankershims—are buried together in Boyle Heights, far across town from their namesake geographical markers. Compared to some of the other historic cemeteries in the city that are entirely mum about where their famous residents are interred, Evergreen Cemetery in Boyle Heights provides visitors a handout. The Lankershim/Van Nuys' burial site is particularly easy to find even without a map. It is marked by a 20-foot-tall obelisk, by far the tallest monument around. Under a single marble monolith, the remains of all four reside. I hope they got along in life. They are certainly close now.

Unlikely as it may seem, also just inside LA's city limits are some ashes of a great man who did not develop property in Southern California. That's Mahatma Gandhi, and it is the only place outside of India where his cremated remains exist. This is at an unexpected pocket of tranquility, mere steps up Sunset Boulevard from the ever-frenetic Pacific Coast Highway and the adjacent beach. In the early 1900s this area served as a movie studio and later as a sand and gravel quarry. Grading was started in preparation for a building development that ultimately folded. The partially completed excavation left a depression that filled up with water from several nearby springs and provided locals with a swimming hole while cattails and reeds competed to make the entire bowl a marsh.

In 1940 a new owner dredged the lake, which made the area useful again for a film set. The owner had visions for much more: a Shangri-La of manicured gardens, tree-covered terraces rising from lakeside, rustic wooden bridges, and emotive rocky outcroppings. He was versed in construction and added a windmill and waterwheel, which would lift water to nourish the slopes of his botanical dream. To live on site while constructing the replica of a 16th century Dutch windmill and waterwheel, he had his two-story boxy houseboat trucked over from Lake Mead, which was filling behind the new Hoover Dam. He and his wife moved into the mill when it was finished and rented the houseboat, Airbnb style, to assorted glitterati. The couple sold the property in

1948, and the new owner planned a 150-room hotel to embrace the lake, but then he had a thrice-repeated dream that changed everything.

He dreamed that a podium appeared in the middle of the lake where ministers of all religions gathered and motivated thousands of listeners with inspirational speeches. Mystically, as the story goes, he connected the next day with Paramahansa Yogananda from the Self-Realization Fellowship Church of All Religions located in Hollywood. With the support of benefactors, Yogananda acquired the property in 1949. While he arranged for the construction of a temple, meditation garden, and a Gandhi memorial, he spent nights on the houseboat. He envisioned a setting that would reflect all aspects of God with beauty, harmony, and peace. Yogananda also invoked a blessing on all future visitors to the shrine, which would include me.

Unannounced, I walked up the short drive from Sunset Boulevard on a Sunday. "Do you have a reservation?" "No, I haven't needed one in the past." "Where's your car?" "At home, I walked." "Welcome." I wondered if I looked like I needed some introspection time. "Thanks."

Within just a few steps, the pocket of tranquility that I remembered displayed itself: flowering shrubs, arching palm trees, manicured walks punctuated periodically with benches surfaced with mosaics depicting the swans and koi, which were soon evident in the water. Across the lake was the houseboat and farther on, the Dutch windmill. Perhaps a hundred other visitors were making peace with themselves, although everyone was as quiet and as serene as the slowly moving swans.

Yogananda believed in a unifying harmony of all faiths, and his Court of Religions displays symbols of five principal religions: a Wheel of Law for Buddhism, a crescent moon and star for Islam, the Om symbol for Hinduism, a Star of David for Judaism, and a cross for Christianity. Not far away, square columns topped with beams supported large gold lotus blossoms and provided a fitting entrance to the Mahatma Ghandi World Peace Memorial. The shrine includes a millennium-old Chinese stone sarcophagus that holds a portion of Gandhi's ashes.

I walked slowly around the lake and sat for a while in several of the secluded niches that were positioned to allow stunning views. Without really trying, I began reflecting on my trek around this young city and its ridiculously brief history compared to Boston or London and especially ranging back 5000 years to when Varanasi, Athens, and Damascus were about LA's current age. What effect was the trek having on me? What effect, if any, was I having on LA? I kept those questions in mind for the remainder of my adventure. Here are a few resulting observations regarding reflection, remembrance, and respect—self-realization.

LA's history is short. So is our collective memory. It is also shallow because Angelenos were not numerous until gold, water, oil, and the entertainment industry made settling here attractive. The land is expensive, and ocean, mountain, and desert barriers limit expansion. So a Houston-like sprawl isn't possible, and without much hesitation we raze rather than respect what came before and tend to destroy what little history we have. Well, almost.

Traveling on foot allowed me to reflect on and grow to respect LA as never before, even tiny things. For instance, I often rode the bus to my starting point for a day's segment. Sometimes that took an hour that included 20 to 30 intervening stops. Passengers exiting before me generally did so through the rear door. I was surprised at first but then heard it again and again when somebody stepped off: "Thank you." What wonderful grace notes of acknowledgment for a tedious and nerve-wrenching job well done.

Another nod to respect comes when Angelenos give and receive directions. Not to bore readers who are less familiar with LA's streets, I will mention just a few, which are either iconic or come in close contact with the city's boundaries. "It's at the corner of Figueroa and Slauson." That statement memorializes General José Figueroa, a governor of California when it belonged to Mexico and Jonathan S. Slauson, a real estate developer at the turn of the 20th century. "Start at its intersection with Lankershim and head west on Chandler until it merges with Van Nuys." (Isaac Lankershim, 19th century mega landowner in the San Fernando Valley; Harry Chandler, owner of the LA Times and businessman extraordinaire; Isaac Newton Van Nuys, Lankershim's son-in-law and real estate magnate.)

"You could take the I-10, but at this time of day it might be faster to take either Wilshire or Pico and exit at Bundy." (Henry Gaylord Wilshire, land developer and socialist who donated a strip of a barley field to LA for a boulevard on the proviso that it would bear his name and that it would exclude a railway and commercial trucking; Pio Pico, the last Mexican governor of California and vast landowner who sold his holdings to Isaac Lankershim; Charles Bundy co-founded the powerful Santa Monica Land and Water Company and developed the present-day Brentwood neighborhood, through which Bundy Drive passes.)

The honoree for some street names may be obscure. For example, consider Hoover Street, which demarcates the original western boundary of El Pueblo de la Reina de los Angeles. After serving as a military surgeon in Napolean's army, Leonce Huber immigrated to California in 1849, changed his name to Hoover and became a well-known vintner. His wine must have been good or plentiful for him to become memorialized in this way.

In other instances, the honorees are obvious. Dale Court and Trigger Street are around the corner from Roy Roger's and Dale Evans's ranch in Chatsworth—horse country. (Trigger was Roy's horse in his many cowboy movies.) Spring Street in downtown LA, by contrast, requires some explanation. The surveyor who was responsible for laying out the city's street grid was infatuated with a young Spanish woman whom he called "mi primavera" (my springtime) for whom he named a downtown street, Calle Primavera. Today, it is Spring Street.

My research discovered other streets that memorialize women. They were often the kin of real estate developers, and those streets are frequently far inside the city limits and thus out of my range of interest along LA's boundaries. One exception is Adelaide Drive, which runs along a bluff that separates Santa Monica from LA near the beach. Two stairways descend sharply from Adelaide across the boundary to reach LA 110 feet below. Adelaide, the daughter of a real estate developer, resided on the street.

In general, the major thoroughfares memorialize men, but not always. For instance, there are two streets that define the city's boundary for miles, La Cienega (see-IN-ee-gah) and Centinela. Who might these major thoroughfares be named for? Nobody. La Cienega means swamp or wetland, which LA had plenty of before meandering streams were channelized. Centinela means sentinel in Spanish, and I found no persuasive opinion regarding how that made it to the map. A rancho and a spring have the same name. Somebody must have been keeping an eye on somebody else.

The origins of other street names are easily understood with the benefit of a little background and simple addition. Olympic Boulevard, originally 10th Street, was renamed shortly after LA hosted the 1932 Olympics. Three blocks south of Olympic and for superstitious reasons,

13th Street never made the maps, rather it became Pico Boulevard. A street parallel to Olympic and Pico that is positioned to be 100th Street is Century Boulevard.

When I started mapping my trek, I had no idea that I would pass seven cemeteries and, even more importantly, that I would find them engaging. The experiences I am going to describe are not nearly so morbid as you might imagine.

I mentioned in Chapter 3 that I like trees, especially ones that have grown without competition and demonstrate their full potential in health, height, and span. I found some of those in parks but more often in cemeteries, especially those with all the grave markers lying flat so the trees have no competition for generating vertical interest.

The cemeteries, by whom they included and excluded, touch on a history of racism and segregation that extended beyond death. In its 150-year existence, Evergreen has accepted over 300,000 burials and is notable in that it never banned African Americans. Nonetheless, it has separate sections for Armenians, Japanese, and Mexicans; and until the Civil Rights era, the cemetery prohibited Chinese burials.

In recent years, a local civic group has created the Evergreen Jogging Path, which follows the 1.4-mile perimeter of the cemetery past shaded benches and exercise stations. Rather than dropping my daypack and trekking poles and jogging, I walked along most of it and wondered if participating in such exercise would postpone the beginning of a long rest on the other side of the fence.

The Odd Fellow Cemetery is nearby, and if its name sounds odd, it is because it was established in the late 1800s by the local lodge of the Independent Order of Odd Fellows, a fraternal organization now over 200 years old. It was an American spinoff of a much older and similarly named organization in England. I asked a worker where the oldest graves were, and I found a number of markers that had the three-linked-rings symbol of the IOOF rising out of the stone and death dates in the late 1800s. At some point the IOOF sold the cemetery, but the name remains along with its serenity.

The resident geese make the Oakwood Memorial Park in Chatsworth, on the far western boundary of LA, a bit less serene. I had skirted this cemetery before while hiking along the Old Santa Susana Stagecoach Road. The southernmost and non-treacherous section of the road had been abandoned years before it and the surrounding ranchos were converted to a cemetery. Signs now warn of geese and coyotes rather than rumbling stagecoaches as the principal hazards. The bronze grave markers lie flat so views of the geese and specimen trees were unimpeded, although looking up to appreciate them risked stepping on annoying goose gifts.

I knew that Fred Astaire and his longstanding dancing partner, Ginger Rogers, were buried at Oakwood Memorial Park. With guidance from the internet, I found his plaque without difficulty. "Fred Astaire. I will always love you. My darling." Several coins nested in the curves of the raised bronze lettering,  which I learned later, notes respect. Astaire's sister, who was his early dance partner, and his mother are buried nearby. I am not sure who called him "my darling."

At some distance across the park, I looked for Ginger's grave unsuccessfully. As I was leaving, two security guards rolled by in a truck. The driver was able to direct me to her plaque. Rogers. Lela 1890-1977. Ginger 1911-1995. Lela was a force of her own—a newspaper reporter, script writer, and movie producer. She was among the first women to enlist in the Marine Corps. Ginger was her only daughter, and they were close in life and remain so in death.

I waved to the guard on the way out and told him that I had found Ginger Rogers plaque. He nodded toward his young partner and told me, "You know, I had to tell him who Ginger Rogers was." Time flies. Fred and Ginger were before my time too, but once seen, their dance routines, which revolutionized the Hollywood musical, are unforgettable feats of creativity, beauty, and athleticism. Fred and Ginger will be dancing on YouTube forever.

The best place for rendezvousing with renowned remains is Forest Lawn Memorial Park, which is ostensibly in Glendale, east of Griffith Park, on the border with Los Angeles, northeast of downtown. A close look at the city boundary at navigatela.lacity.org shows that the entrance is in Glendale, but the boundary cuts obliquely across the park with two thirds of the cemetery in Los Angeles. Is anybody concerned that their father might be buried in LA and their mother, by his side, might be resting in Glendale? Here is a thought for mystery writers. What if the city limits cut right across a single burial plot and its occupant was disinterred for forensic reasons? Which city would have jurisdiction? Fortunately, I did not confront these consuming questions until after I had walked through this beautiful park.

Hubert Eaton moved to Los Angeles in 1911 after failing to parlay his chemistry degree into a career in silver mining. He found a job selling grave plots on commission to mourning families at the recently opened Forest Lawn Cemetery. He had a plan and by 1917 had taken over management of the 300-acre property. He renamed it Forest Lawn Memorial Park to rid it of the stigma associated with the word "cemetery." He soon realized that in the near term he was not going to make much money selling plots only to bereaving families, so he decided to make his property sufficiently attractive so that well-to-do families would buy plots far in advance of actually occupying them.

Along this line of thinking, he eliminated all the traditional gravestones, obelisks, weeping angels, and other above-ground indicators of sadness and replaced them with bronze grave markers laid flat. Not only did this make lawn maintenance much easier, but it also turned the steep hillsides and scattered trees into a park, which he developed to the hilt. Eaton, not one for understatement, called himself "The Builder" and collected original artwork from afar and commissioned replicas of famous sculptures that made the park a giant a sculpture garden divided into separate areas. These included ones featuring a replica of Michaelangelo's *David* and one with several statues of Jesus.

The Little Mermaid, who sits pensively on a rock aside Copenhagen's harbor, soon had her double contemplating water in a shallow pool inside the park's front gates (in Glendale). Nearby is the florist shop. The Builder also acquired a 13-foot-tall sculpture of George Washington that was originally intended to grace the rotunda in the US Capitol Building. Various burial areas have soothing names including Whispering Pines, Haven of Peace, Mercy, Tranquility, and Brotherly Love. On a larger scale, the park includes a reproduction of a 17th century Scottish stone chapel and a museum that has rotating exhibits as well as a permanent collection of marble and bronze sculptures. At the far end of the museum is the gift shop, where small reproductions of the sculptures as well as other memorabilia are available for souvenir hunters. From the museum parking lot and its retaining wall (Eaton might say ramparts) situated on the highest elevation of the Park, an unobstructed vista of North Hollywood and the distant San Gabrial Mountains, including Mt. Lukens, unfolds. An Easter morning sunrise service is held there. Weddings as well as funerals take place in various chapels.

Then there is the Grand Mausoleum, a towering cathedral-like structure. In its Memorial Court, a 30-foot stained-glass reproduction of Leonardo's *The Last Supper* fills the wall, and immediately below, occupants are buried in the floor, Westminster Abby fashion. Only "immortals", selected by a secret committee, are invited to rest there. Michael Jackson is somewhere nearby but cloistered from the public. William Mulholland is also in proximity.

Eaton's plan for preselling cemetery plots was immensely successful. For nearly 40 years, it was also California's most popular tourist attraction and considered to be the country's first theme park before Disneyland opened in 1955. Walt Disney and Eaton were good friends, and the idea of a park with themed areas clearly crossed over from The Builder's Memorial Park to Disney's Magic Kingdom. Disney, along with myriad other notables from the entertainment industry are buried there. The staff is cagey and will not reveal the exact location of your favorite stars, but if you feel the urge to visit, no worry. The clerk in the gift shop told me, "Check on the internet." It is no secret where The Builder is buried—in the Grand Mausoleum's Memorial Court.

Before he settled in for good at the foot of *The Last Supper*, Eaton developed five other Forest Lawn Memorial Parks in the Los Angeles area. The other one that was on my path is about five miles west across Griffith Park (and entirely in LA). I could look down on it the day I thought I might get arrested atop the decommissioned Toyon Canyon landfill. Later I walked in. Forest Lawn Memorial Park—Hollywood Hills has a road that meanders up the same mountainside that gives Griffith Park its varied terrain and gives the park a rural feeling. The vistas are not as stunning as those in the original park, and the glitterati buried there are not quite so numerous or glittery in toto. Everybody has their favorites, and they are equally hard to find without guidance.

I was, however, standing in front of a retaining wall and glanced down. The marble plaque read, STAN LAUREL. 1890-1965. A MASTER OF COMEDY. HIS GENIUS IN THE ART OF HUMOR BROUGHT GLADNESS TO THE WORLD HE LOVED.

Overcoming my surprise, I looked back up the hillside to see the Court of Liberty looming every bit as ostentatiously as any of the themed areas in Glendale. Here stand statues of Washington and Jefferson and beyond them the Birth of Liberty, the largest historical mosaic in the US. Ten million pieces of Venetian glass are spread along this 162-foot long, 28-foot high, mural. The mural depicts 25 scenes from 17th and 18th century American history, and it is hard to comprehend its magnitude and complexity without seeing it. In the meantime, trust me. The Builder came through again.

Another remarkable feature of this Memorial Park is its full-scale replica of Boston's Old North Church. What's the logic of it being there? Who knows? But along with the other features, it certainly removed my mind from any notion of death.

And hey, it's Hollywood—anything but boring.

CHAPTER 9

BOREDOM?

I was asked several times, "Did you walk the *entire* way, even the boring stretches?" "Yes, I walked every inch because I wanted to say honestly that I did."

True, there were several of the ten-mile segments, often along flat, straight commercial streets, where I had not identified any potential points of interest from my maps or "best of" lists. Maybe I am easy to amuse and hard to bore because I made as many discoveries and had as much fun on these segments as on any of the others, including the attraction-dense, medal-winning areas.

Before starting the trek, I had identified well over 300 potential points of interest where I planned to stop—an average of one attraction per mile walked. There were, however, two consecutive ten-mile segments that looked on paper to be attraction-sparse. Those sections started near Los Angeles International Airport and headed northeast toward Inglewood before turning south toward San Pedro. On this stretch I had pinpointed only two potential stops.

So one day I set off to walk double my normal distance to push through this bland portion of my trip, wondering if any surprises might be in store. Indeed, there were.

In my haste to knock out those 21 miles, I rushed past a potentially interesting stop within the first mile and later kicked myself for not thoroughly investigating it. It was a low brick building set back from a major intersection. Big metal letters on the windowless front wall indicated that this was a Los Angeles Department of Water and Power Distribution Center. I wondered if it was water or electricity that was being distributed. The front door was open, and immediately inside was a woman scowling at me from behind her desk. In diminished light to one side stood several workmen in hard hats and reflective vests. The body language of all suggested that I was not welcome. Behind Ms. Frowny, a wall of electrical panels, switches, and gauges provided the answer to my basic question, but everybody's unwelcoming postures intimidated me from saying, "Hi, I am not a terrorist, just a curious wayfarer. Tell me, where is the electricity coming from? How many volts? Where is it going?" Also, I was focused on walking another 20 miles, so I hightailed it back to the sidewalk and pressed ahead. On reflection, I regretted that decision. I should have given each worker my *Walking the Line* business card, explained my trek, and asked my questions. Over the 40-plus years that I have lived in LA, I had driven by that building a hundred times, and never before had I seen the door open. This time, expediency won out over opportunity. "Slow down, Roy, take it *all* in. It's the journey, not the destination.," I repeated to myself as I marched on, and with each step, the decision to go back became progressively harder.

Then other attractions gained my attention.

I passed a corner shopping center with an overhead sign indicating D & H Plaza, beneath which was a large graphic labeled "Wings and Pot." Sure, I had passed a number of cannabis shops on previous days, and this sign seemed to indicate one more, but what extra buzz might come from wings at this farmacy? Much smaller letters across the bottom of the sign clarified the promotion: Chicken Wings and Loaded Potatoes.

Other ambiguous or ironic signs caught my eye that day. These included Car and Bike Wash, and Visitors Park Outside. Did the first one mean motorbikes or bicycles? I never thought about taking either one to a car wash. Did the second one imply that residents could park in the living room?

While I am on the subject of ambiguous and and amusinigns amusing signs, I am going to digress momentarily and note ones that I encountered on other days. These included:

- MOOSE and SENIOR ZONE (Neither had an explanation nor were they in close proximity to each other.)
- DO NOT DRIVE ON BIKE PATH (Okay.)
- NO UNAUTHORIZED ENTRY INTO THE LOS ANGELES ZOO OR ANIMAL ENCLOSURES ALLOWED (The latter part seems intuitive.)
- BARTENDER PARKING ONLY (This must be a perk to keep their car from being hit by drunk patrons.)
- PLEASE, NO TRESSPOOPING (A canine silhouette the potential offender.)
- TOYS, GAMES, WHOOPIE CUSHIONS (No potential offender was identified.)
- NO VANDALISM (Darn it.)
- Several other signs warned of natural hazards:
- BEWARE OF ALLIGATOR (I couldn't see over the wall, so not sure if this was a joke.)
- CAUTION, RATTLESNAKES and BEWARE OF COYOTES IN THIS AREA (I'm quite certain these were legitimate.)
- PERSONS HAVING CURRENTLY ACTIVE DIARRHEA OR WHO HAVE HAD ACTIVE DIARRHEA IN THE PAST 14 DAYS SHALL NOT BE ALLOWED TO ENTER THE POOL/SPA WATER (Thank you, but what is inactive diarrhea?)
- PLEASE STAY 20 TACOS APART (These sidewalk stickers were near a food truck—practical advice during the COVID-19 pandemic.)

- THROWN OBJECTS, SKATE/HOVER BOARDS OR DRONES WITHIN 100 YARDS OF PONY RIDE AREA ARE PROHIBITED. (That seemed reasonable, but this Griffith Park concession had been closed for several years.)

I say it again, automobilistas miss so much.

With my pedestrian advantage, I also studied the artistry of manhole covers and the shape, color, and formatting of street signs. I will detail my observations of these in the chapter on infrastructure. I have a sense that utility poles, light fixtures, and storm gratings are also fascinating, but I came to those realizations well into the trek, so I will save an exploration of these industrial artistic expressions for a future adventure.

Now I will return to the description of my planned 21-mile day. Not far beyond where I was advised to park outside, I marveled at a perfect image of Americana. Atop each Golden Arch of a McDonalds, a seagull stood guard. An American flag fluttered in the foreground, its pole topped with an eagle, wings spread. Clear blue sky filled the background. Noon was approaching, and I felt a Big Mac beckoning, but I walked on, hoping to find "local" fare here in LA's Hyde Park neighborhood.

I did. I almost past it because there was no indication from the sidewalk of what goods or services the shop, named Crustees, provided. So, following my resolve to go more slowly, I went inside. It was a family-owned quick-serve restaurant specializing in on-site cooking and baking—chicken pot pie, turkey chili, seafood gumbo, jalapeno cheddar cornbread, five-inch fruit pies and cobblers, and banana pudding, among other delectables. The place was modern and spotless. I had some gumbo and cornbread. Delicious.

Next I passed through Park Mesa Heights, the neighborhood where my path turned from northeast to south to continue along the convoluted border leading to the Shoestring and San Pedro. Why Park Mesa Heights is so named eludes me, because although there was a park in the area, neither a mesa nor any other promontory was evident. This was South Los Angeles, Nipsey Hussle's neighborhood and the site of a rare point of interest on this stretch that my research had identified. Filling the wall of a Fat Burger outlet called, "The Last Great Hamburger Stand," was a mural of Nipsey. I went inside and had an "Original," which was good but not worth repeating soon.

I asked the cashier what the connection was between the restaurant and Nipsey's huge image on the wall. She told me to go outside and around the corner for an explanation. There, behind a tall and locked metal fence was a low building set back from the street. The sign said, Neighborhood Nip Foundation. I couldn't discern whether this was an off day for them or if the place was permanently closed.

I knew that, in addition to being a famous rapper, Nipsey was an entrepreneur and community activist before he was gunned down in 2019 at age 33. My later research turned up that Nipsey wanted to inspire other young Black men and that he scorned gun violence in his music and community activism. He even performed with rappers who were members of rival gangs to seek appeasement. An overhanging roof protects the Fat Burger mural from rain and somewhat from the sun, so it should remain a memorial to this interesting character for a long time.

Down the street, I heard a recycling center in full operation before I looked through the gate and saw several pick-ups and vans lined up. Drivers were tossing huge trash bins and bags filled with sorted glass, plastic, and aluminum containers into the center's bins where they were weighed. It was too noisy to ask the workers about the destiny of the recyclables. I did ask one seller where his chest-high plastic barrel of glass bottles came from. "Restaurants." I asked another about his two equally large containers of aluminum beer cans. "Mostly from home, plus from my father and brother." He seemed sober. As I walked on, I wondered about his relatives.

The best surprise of the day was stumbling on the Sims Library of Poetry, a bright blue one-story box with an inviting canopied courtyard on the side. Painted letters on a low sidewalk wall indicated "POETRY LIVES HERE." Poet-professor-owner Hiram Sims was standing outside. He told me that he had earned degrees in creative and professional writing from the University of Southern California where he began to teach creative writing. His students complained that they did not have access to poetry books, so he started bringing some to class in a suitcase. His "library" expanded to shelves in his garage and then to its current

location, which is home to 10,000 volumes of poetry, three of which are his own creations. He hosts poetry readings nearly every Saturday evening and advocates that poetry be heard, not merely read.

I asked him how he became interested in poetry. "It was in middle school. I wrote a poem for a girl. With that alone, she went with me for two weeks. I learned that poetry softens the hearts of women." Hiram noted that his was the first Black-owned poetry library in California. It seemed to me that Hiram could probably make anybody fall in love with verse.

Other bookish attractions would pop up from time to time along my walk and surprise me and always made me smile. I would stop to admire the design and peruse the contents of these roller-bag-sized cabinets mounted on sidewalk-adjacent posts. A small metal plate on each announced, Little Free Library. Take a book. Share a book. This worldwide movement for exchanging books and building community started in 2009 in Wisconsin when Todd Bol placed the structure simulating a one-room schoolhouse in his front yard to honor his mother, a teacher and avid reader. Now he runs a nonprofit organization with a worldwide reach. Tens of thousands of LFLs have sprouted up in over 100 countries. Their vision includes this statement. "We believe all people are empowered when the opportunity to discover a personally relevant book to read is not limited by time, space, or privilege."

The cabinets I found all had glass doors with their frames and side walls covered with paint ranging from whimsical floral designs to rather sedate monotones. Roofing material varied from corrugated metal to artificial grass to bamboo to painted wood. The books inside were equally wide-ranging in size, shape, and topic. On LFLs website, I learned that librarian wannabees can buy a completely assembled cabinet in a variety of styles. They also come in do-it-yourself kits.

Who could be against such a great idea? Apparently, some people find these oversized birdhouses offensive because they gentrify urban neighborhoods and "steal patronage from existing public library branches." Some towns have had to reconsider their building codes, because in at least one instance the LFL was considered an illegal "separate structure." Wow.

Well, I guess if LFLs can stir controversy, here is their cousin, who seems so nice and innocent too, but who knows? Along my entire trek, I discovered only one Free Little Art Gallery, but I suspect that they will become more common as the concept catches on. The FLAG I encountered was wider and not quite as tall as most of the LFLs I had seen. It also had a transparent plastic roof, which allowed more light to enter the gallery.

The interior was the dollhouse version of an art museum—a bench and several miniature visitors viewing smaller-than-postcard-size works of art arranged on easels and wall ledges. These included a portrait of a red-haired woman, a painting of a bright yellow hibiscus on a dappled green background, and several abstracts. On the hardwood floor, a stand supported a small green ceramic cup. Wording above the door encouraged visitors to "MAKE ART, ADD ART, ENJOY ART, TAKE ART." Another sign said, "PLEASE DO NOT TAKE THE EASELS OR PEOPLE."

Though walking was its own reward, it sure was nice to get some culture as a bonus. I can't wait for a curbside box labeled Little Free Symphony. Need a reprieve from street noise? Open LFS's door and enjoy some Beethoven, loud enough to drown out any traffic sounds.

There was plenty of traffic noise and not much to look at along a stretch of Western Avenue in the Shoestring. Overgrown shrubs covered the curbside embankment and shielded whatever elements of civilization resided on the far side. Boring? Before I could answer myself, I came across another "by the way" attraction. Centered in a large shrub covered with bright red berries was a Toyota wheel cover—a medallion. The central Toyota logo was surrounded by five small holes for the lug nuts, and radiating from there were wide spokes alternating with open triangles connecting the hub to the rim. The combination of bright colors and the symmetry of the disk versus the randomness of the plant was striking. Had somebody composed this? If so, congratulations. Or had the wheel cover fallen off a car, bounced down the pavement, and landed here by chance? Contemplating this, I walked on with a spring in my step.

Another art form that I encountered was actually in the street, sometimes parked curbside, sometimes zooming along on its way to elsewhere. Los Angeles is car-centric, and the attitude of many here is that you are what you drive (compared to Washington D.C., where I understand that you are where you dine). The Olympic motto for athletes is "Faster, Higher, Stronger." For many LA drivers, the motto is "Faster, Bigger, Newer." That is why vintage vehicles stand out. I sensed that there were more along the city's boundaries than I typically see in its more congested areas. They always surprised me and drew my smile.

Even if you traced my steps, it is unlikely that you would see the same ones I did, but any sighting is guaranteed to break the monotony of what might be imagined as a boring walk.

For example, a red, rakish sports car parked in a bungalow's front yard had a license plate that nailed its identity. "54 MG TF."

A barge-sized, chrome-laden Cadillac from the 1940s sat curbside with its front windows down at 7 am. Maybe the owner, not in sight, considered that theft was not an issue because nobody could afford to fill it with gas.

I talked to the owners of a restored 1960 VW beetle and a 1948 Chevy, which included chrome "eyebrows" over the headlights and a windshield visor that looked like a misplaced spoiler.

There were some lowriders. One such pickup at curbside had air in its tires, but they lifted the vehicle insufficiently for its running boards and front bumper to clear the pavement. Maybe it had hydraulics that lifted it when it was time to roll. A 1963 Chevy Impala certainly did. It was parked well away from the curb on a quiet residential street as I walked up from behind. The front bumper must have been nearly touching the pavement because the rear end was high enough on its trick hydraulics that I could easily see the glistening chrome on the differential, axles, and springs. I chatted with the guy who had just finished washing this fully restored gem and asked him if the car could dance. "Of course, want to see it?" "Sure." He leaned through the driver's door and flipped some control to make the front and rear ends alternately pop up and down.

I asked, "Can I get a video clip of that?"

"Probably not, the owner is sitting there on the porch."

"Oh. Hi there."

He had been quietly watching. I walked partway up the driveway to talk to him. He was retired, not in particularly good health, and loved street cruising. A statewide ban on such fun had just recently been lifted so he was keen on being able to legally show off for the first time since 1988.

Just inside the city line along the Shoestring, I came across a four-foot-tall velociraptor, a five-foot-tall ice cream sundae with a cherry on top, and an even taller gold replica of the Eiffel Tower, all stationed on the sidewalk. The sign on the adjacent door said, "PLATINUM PROP HOUSE, LIFE SIZE STATUES. THEME PARTY PROPS."

I said, "Whoopee, another 'by the way.' This should be good." From the lobby, I could peek into the warehouse. "Mind if I have a look around?" "Not at all, go ahead."

Thousands of props were packed together with barely enough room to squirm between them. For somebody planning a wedding with a Western theme, PPH has horses, corrals, and wagon wheels to set the tone. How about a corporate awards dinner? Superheroes including Mutant Ninja Turtles, Spiderman, Superman, and Batman stand ready. An after-Emmy party? Six-foot tall Oscars would look great guarding the front door. Prom? Rent what you like: candy canes, a British phone booth or two, mermaids, giraffes, Tin Man, Captain Hook, gasoline pumps, giant popcorn boxes.

Two in-house technicians will custom make any prop that PPH doesn't have already. They also touch up all the props on return from an event to have them in tip top shape before they grace the next event. They deliver and pick up, which is good because they can lay a giraffe on its side, whereas transporting a real one is problematic. PPH is located in an unlikely spot, pinched between the Harbor Freeway and an intersection with service stations on three corners. Cars whizzed by in all directions, oblivious to the chimps and pumpkins inside PPH waiting for prime time.

Over the day, several people asked about my trekking poles. The most common comment was, "Going skiing?" When I explained to one curious woman that they aided balance and helped stepping on and off curbs, she said that she was going to get a pair for her sister, who was marginally ambulatory and was not getting enough exercise. It made me feel good to be an ambassador of ambulation.

In the early afternoon, I saw mothers walking their grade-schoolers home. I was envious of the spring in the kids' steps, but then too, they had not walked 16 miles (42,132 steps) already. This distance was the longest for any day on my trek and, excluding training for and running three marathons (ugh!), it was the most I had ever traveled by foot in one day. It gave me pause to appreciate good shoes—broken in but not worn out.

To emphasize the point about wearing good shoes, here is what a young man at a bus stop related as our conversation turned from trekking poles to shoes. "I bought these at a garage sale for just $9. They're too big, and after running in them twice I got plantar fasciitis, which has not gone away." Thank you, good shoes and good sense.

I had planned to cover 21 miles, but this "boring" stretch was full of interest, so my speed was curtailed, and I ran out of both time and steam. I decided to leave the rest of this segment for another day. Before hopping onto the bus, I came across two small ironies.

The first was a fenced-off building in disrepair. Painted letters that were peeling off the front of the building identified it as the "Los Angeles Racing Pigeon Club." Below them, in far more recent spray paint, someone had scrawled, Never give up. No way to know if the two messages were related.

The second was a large sign towering over a corner shopping center. My Vermont Market was underwritten with Healthy Produce-Liquor-Beer-Wine. Confusing? Yes. I should have gone inside to see if that was all they sold. Boring? No.

CHAPTER 10

GRIFFITH PARK

I t is now time to present the second Hot Spot award. "The envelope, please." (The crowd quiets in anticipation.) "The silver medal goes to… Griffith Park." (Complete silence. Pause. No applause.) Apparently the honoree requires some explanation.

Griffith J. Griffith was his real name. Maybe his mother thought that by so naming him she would double her chances of gaining his attention when she hollered "Griffith." In later years he called himself Colonel and liked others to do the same although nobody can find any military records to support the implied claim. Regardless, his philanthropy stands tall in the history of altruism among Angelenos. And how many philanthropists do you know who served prison time for attempted murder? The Colonel did. Details later.

By size alone, Griffith Park deserves recognition. Its irregular shape is not nearly as crazy as LA's and measures roughly three miles from top to bottom and two-and-a-half miles from side to side. At 4310 acres, it is as large as the following well-known municipal parks *combined*: New York's Central Park, San Francisco's Golden Gate Park, San Diego's Balboa Park, Lincoln Park in Chicago, and Hermann Park in Houston.

It is also large enough that several of its well-known attractions are farther than a mile inside the LA city limits and, therefore, out of bounds for my trek and not taken into consideration when selecting the Hot Spot award winners. These are the iconic Hollywood sign, Griffith Observatory, Bronson Caves, Fern Dell, and Greek Theatre, which is a 6,000-seat amphitheater and performance venue.

I have previously described several attractions within the park that do contribute to Griffith Park's silver medal award. These were the old zoo and the Toyon Canyon landfill. Some other points of interest confirm Griffith Park's appeal to urban adventurists.

Compared to most city parks across America, large portions of Griffith Park are mountainous, untamed wilderness, sufficiently so that P-22, a mountain lion, lived there unobtrusively for over 10 years. Rather sure that I would not be pounced on, I went horseback riding one morning, the first time in almost 40 years. Aboard Mouse, I ambled with the trail guide, Tiffany, and three other riders first across a narrow bridge (load limit six horses) that passed over the Los Angeles River and then through a tunnel under the 134 Freeway. This led us from the stables in Glendale to cross the city boundary into Los Angeles and Griffith Park's Oak Canyon.

Almost 250 years earlier, Juan Bautista de Anza and his entourage of 300 people and 1000 head of livestock rode and walked along here on the first overland colonizing expedition into California from Spanish-controlled Mexico. Months later, they completed their journey and established a presidio (fortification) and a mission in what was to become San Francisco. But for me, an hour in the saddle with bright sunshine and a little dust was enough. It was plenty of time to consider horseback vs. foot transportation and acknowledge my preference for the latter, with one exception.

I have an affection for miniature trains, and Griffith Park is close to my heart in this regard.

A bronze statue of GJG stands proudly at the main entrance to the park, and not far inside is the entrance to the Griffith Park Southern Pacific Railroad. The locomotive was a replica of an early steam engine complete with a cowcatcher and a funnel-shaped smokestack. The cars were big enough for an adult and child to sit side by side. (I was by myself but did not sense any weird looks.)

Once out of the station, the train passed close behind the Colonel's statue, looped near the modern and heavily trafficked Riverside Drive, and then into the woods and down Main Street of Griffith Gulch. The saloon, bank, and hospital were on the right. I wondered if there was any irony in their proximity to one another. On the left and farther on, the blacksmith's and undertaker's shingles were followed by designations for the general store, barber, sheriff, and hotel. I mused about the practicality of a train track running down the middle of Main Street, but I did appreciate the absence of automobiles and understood that they had not yet been invented. This miniature railroad was in the southeast corner of the park. Catercorner across and an hour's walk away were the other train-related attractions.

First in line was the Disney Carolwood Barn. Walt and his wife lived for many years on a large property on Carolwood Drive in the tony neighborhood of Holmby Hills. The estate was large enough that he had room for a one-eighth-scale live-steam model railroad that circled the entire property and also looped through smaller areas several times. In one hillside section, the layout was going to interfere with his wife's sunny flower garden. No problem. Walt tunneled under it. He also built a replica of the barn from his childhood home in Missouri, and this served as his workshop and gathering spot for friends who shared his love of trains. After his death, his family arranged for the barn,

which Walt had described as his "happy place," to be donated to the Los Angeles Live Steamers Railroad Museum, where he had been a founding member.

You may be thinking, "What kind of a second-rate attraction is this? Maybe I will skip ahead."

Well, it was only one of two attractions on my entire trek that I had to wait in line to visit.

Admittedly the Carolwood Barn is open only one Sunday a month, and it was a beautiful day. Along with families and young couples, I waited for 20 minutes to get through the outer gate surrounding the property and then another 30 minutes to enter the barn. Inside, historic photographs document the Carolwood Pacific Railroad's construction and operation along with photos of Walt wearing bib overalls and an engineer's hat. His tools are there along with a sizable, small-scale model railroad layout and all sorts of train memorabilia. After visiting the barn, I had a clear idea why somebody, as fixated on trains and as wealthy as Walt, would want to build a full-scale historic railroad. He did. Now it circles Disneyland.

The other place where I waited in line was a quarter mile away. The Carolwood Barn and the LA Live Steamers Railroad Museum share the same surrounding chain-link fence, but to get from one entry to the other, everybody walks outside the property and down the street. We waited there for another 20 minutes to catch a ride that made two big loops, one of which ran right past the Carolwood Barn, where the entry queue had grown even longer.

The locomotives are diesel replicas, and the Live Steam layout is a much smaller gauge than the one at the park's front entry. This meant that all we passengers—self-certified to be at least 36 inches tall and less than 350 pounds—straddled flat cars with our feet hanging out a bit. Before the train left the station, the conductor was on the platform taking photos of families settling in. I handed him my cell phone and asked him to take my picture. "Just you?" "Yep." I was certainly an outlier among the kids, parents, and grandparents, but his facial expression did not change, and off we went. Trestles, bridges, a mining tunnel, a ghost town, and the Carolwood Barn surrounded by a line of Disney fans. Nice breeze. It felt good to sit.

Then I hoofed it out the gate to Travel Town, another quarter of a mile down the street. This outdoor museum displays 43 railcars and behemoth locomotives from the age of steam, roughly 1880-1930. Some of them came from Gene Autry's ranch after much of it burned. I cannot think of another museum where visitors can circle the collection on a miniature train. Its locomotive was identical to the first one

in the park, but these passenger cars had bench seats and canopies. When this train ride was over, I walked among the locomotives to a barn where some dusty old street vehicles were bursting with history. Cobwebs and chipped paint emphasized their age. The conveyances included a Carnation milk delivery truck, a Railway Express truck and platform wagon, and a Los Angeles Gas and Electric buckboard.

I already mentioned Gene Autry (1907-98). Even if you have never heard of this cowboy crooner, you have. At least you have heard him sing his signature song, "Back in the Saddle Again," along with these Christmas stalwarts: "Rudolph, the Red-Nosed Reindeer", "Frosty the Snowman", and "Here Comes Santa Claus," which he penned himself. He had a stellar career as a singer, song writer, and actor first on radio, then on film, and later on TV. He was also a businessman who seemed to carefully manage and enjoy his wealth.

As his money multiplied, Autry began collecting Western memorabilia (along with radio stations and a Major League Baseball team). He hoped to build a museum of cowboy heritage on his ranch north of Los Angeles, but after a fire swept through, his dream came to fruition in Griffith Park, just inside LA's boundary line. The museum was founded in 1988 as the Gene Autry Western Heritage Museum and became home not only for Autry's collection of Western memorabilia and art but also for donations from his friends and other Western media stars. It is now known as the Autry Museum of the American West, and its scope has broadened. Its mission statement is now to bring together "the stories of all peoples of the American West, connecting the past with the present to inspire our shared future." It has well over a half million cultural objects and works of art that include one of the largest and most important collections of Native American materials. The museum is uniquely positioned to record and preserve important elements of regional history. It is always fun to visit, and I learn more every time.

From the Autry, I crossed the street and a large surface parking lot to arrive at the LA Zoo. The parking lot site itself is noteworthy for several reasons. In the immediate vicinity in 1774, de Anza and his entourage camped en route to establishing a chain of Spanish missions terminating in San Francisco. Then in 1912 the Griffith Park Aerodrome opened and became the home for a group of aviation factories and schools. The area that is presently the zoo parking lot and the site of the Autry Museum was perfect for such endeavors because the LA River, unpaved at that time, periodically flooded and washed the site flat. Beacon Hill, a nearby and vista-rich destination for modern-day hikers, derived its name because the airport's signal light topped it off. In 1946, the airport closed, and the city erected 750 Quonset huts to house returning veterans and their families. Few sites in La La Land have been repurposed this many times.

Inside the zoo, I always love watching the crazy meerkats. They look like masked bandits scooting in and out of their tunnels, but then they act so innocent sitting on their haunches and looking all around with their hands draped in front of their chins. I also marvel at how the flamingoes can stand on one leg, tuck their head under a wing, and take a nap.

What I would really like to do is revert to my teenage years and attend high school at the LA Unified School District's Zoo Magnet, which is located only a brief meerkat scamper from the entrances of both the Autry and the zoo. This is one of only six high schools nationally that partners with a zoo. Ninth graders start out working with and caring for domesticated animals, which include alpacas, pigs, donkeys, and goats. These activities take place on the parent North Hollywood High campus's eight-acre agriculture area. By 11th grade, students are studying animal behavior and zoology taught by LA zookeepers and docents. They also enrich their studies in art history and anthropology in collaboration with resources at the Autry Museum. As high school seniors, they become assistant zookeepers and are involved in all the tasks that are safe for them and the animals. Many students eventually end up in human health science or veterinary careers. I would volunteer to help with the meerkats.

Up to this point, the activities I have described in Griffith Park need some sort of admission ticket or at least permission. So does a round of golf on either of the championship courses. There is so much more, however, that is ad lib. This includes picnicking, hiking and mountain biking (53 miles of trails), badminton, tennis, soccer (seven fields), baseball, soft ball, and children's playgrounds. Alas, the pony rides and a vintage merry-go-round have closed in recent years.

For history buffs, there's even more. Two bronze plaques in the park record changing times. One is set in a picnic area close to the LA River and commemorates the aforementioned de Anza's overland colonizing expedition into California. The other is near the clubhouse for the Wilson and Harding golf courses. It is labeled "THE BIRTH OF THE CURSE" and resonates with baseball fanatics.

On a day in January, 1920, Babe Ruth was playing a round and was met on the course by the New York Yankees' manager, who sought and obtained Ruth's permission to be traded from the world champion Red Sox to the Yankees. This proved to be a painful day indeed for Boston fans, who had reveled in Red Sox World Series victories in 1915, 1916, and 1918 with Ruth's contributions (and, as it turned out, would not have this reason to celebrate again until 2004). Ruth and the Yankees dominated Major League Baseball for many years after the trade.

I hope that I have convinced you that Griffith Park deserves an attraction-dense medal. How did this wonderful public resource come about? Griffith J. Griffith (1850-1919) immigrated penniless and without prospects to the United States from Wales at age 15. By 1873 he was managing a publishing company in San Francisco. Soon after he became the mining correspondent for a local newspaper, and as a side gig, prepared confidential mining reports for high rollers. By using that information to invest on his own, GJG became wealthy.

By 1882, he had moved to Los Angeles and bought 4,000 acres of an original Mexican land grant, the Rancho Los Feliz. For a time, he raised ostriches—their feathers were quite the thing for ladies' hats at the time. In 1896, he was apparently feeling flush and donated three fourths of the Rancho to Los Angeles for a park, and the city leaders named the park for him. Later, GJG gave the city another, adjacent 1,000 acres. Today, Los Feliz is the name of an adjacent residential neighborhood.

Despite his largess, Griffith was not well-liked. H e lived at the same time as movers and shakers such as William Mulholland, Isaac Newton Van Nuys, Phineas Banning, Henry Huntington, Harry Chandler, and Moses Sherman. They were shaping LA to their will (and they all left their surnames on streets, neighborhoods, or both). GJG likely had some contact with them, but many people found the Colonel overdressed, pompous, and egomaniacal.

Unknown to most, GJG was an alcoholic. This came to light when, in a demented rage, he shot his wife in the face, intending to kill her. She survived, and GJG spent nearly two years in San Quentin to compensate for his misdeed.

A few years later, he offered Los Angeles a third large gift, this time money, to build an amphitheater and an observatory in the park. Considering it a bribe to buy a better reputation, the Park Commission

objected, went to court to block the gift, and won. But after GJG's
death from liver disease (surprise!), the money from his estate passed
to the city. This resulted in the opening of the Greek Theater in 1929
and the Griffith Observatory and Planetarium in 1935. Although
not as densely packed as attractions in Griffith Park, a lot of other
amusements skirt the LA city limits, and I wanted to try them all.

CHAPTER 11

FUN

It's hard to do pushups with boxing gloves on; but after ten reps, we were given a break and told to drop down, support our weight on our forearms, and perform a minute's worth of plank. Then without pause, do ten more pushups, then another minute of plank, followed by repeating the cycle two more times. I managed all this pretty well but heard some gasping and groaning down the line. This was the way my boxing lesson ended.

I had walked past the Sunland Fight Club several months earlier and had now returned for an evening lesson. I had no idea what to expect, but that is part of any adventure. Vahan, the instructor, wore some of his credentials—sizable scars—on his forehead and cheek. For starters, the four other students, all two to five decades my junior, and I jogged around the large, matted area. This lasted at least ten minutes, and several times as I passed by Vahan, he asked me how I was doing. "Fine." Then with each additional lap we limbered up a separate set of joints, first fingers, then wrists and so forth up our arms and then down our legs with high stepping, heel kicking, side walking, toes only, and heels only. Then we shadow-boxed while jogging a couple more laps.

One time as I passed him, Vahan asked me if I wanted some water. "No thanks." Several laps later he asked my age. I told him. Impressed or aghast, his scars were expressionless.

I think jump roping came next. I hadn't tried this for eons and couldn't make the rope hum like Rocky did. Rather I had several resets. The time needed to untangle the cord from my feet mercifully allowed me to catch my breath for a second. Then we donned gloves and punched heavy bags for at least five minutes with one fist, then five more with the other, then five more with combos. I wasn't making my bag swing as widely as the other students, all of whom had been there before. My arms were so tired I had trouble holding them up, that is until I realized that the Nazo Boxing stencil on the bag could be the face of anybody who had ever annoyed me. Bam, bam, with renewed vigor.

Then came the final pushup/plank agony combo. Vahan took off before we could tell him what we thought of him. I asked the student who was closest in age to me if he had visions of punching vexatious villains while on the bag. "I'm past that, but yes." Another student told me, "You know, Vahan was complimenting you the whole time we were doing planks." "No, I didn't hear him." "When we were struggling, he said, 'Look to the left'." He was taunting them to emulate the old man.

Any vision of future glory in the ring, however, was blunted the second morning afterward when my shoulder muscles and abs were aching in response to the unaccustomed strenuous activity—DOMS, delayed onset muscle soreness. At least my legs weren't aching as they had after descending Mt. Lukens. They were in decent shape from all my walking.

Here are five other amusements I sampled. Decide which one might be the most appealing to you. At the end, I'll give you my opinion and explain why.

Along Foothill Boulevard in Sylmar, one of LA's northernmost neighborhoods, I passed a low, windowless building situated on the edge of a park. The street-side label cryptically indicated "Discovery Cube." That piqued my curiosity, and since I was on a terrestrial voyage of discovery, I ventured in along with a steady stream of families with kids of all ages. What a discovery—the coolest science and technology museum ever.

"Hands on" was obviously the mantra guiding the designers of the exhibits. All of them were interactive and sized for children, but I had a blast too, interacting with the exhibits myself and watching the other kids happily increasing their knowledge of and appreciation for science and technology. Nobody seemed to notice that I did not have a child in tow as I played hockey goalie and tried to stop slap shots coming at me from one of three holes in the wall. In another area, we assembled race cars from bins of wheels and bodies and then tested their speeds against an electronic timer. My seniority counted for nothing in constructing the fastest car.

Two exhibits were insidiously sly in teaching good habits. The first was sponsored by the LA Department of Sanitation. A long conveyor belt carried a steady stream of simulated garbage for the contestant to sort and place into separate bins for recycling, compost, or land fill— all against a timer. The second was a scaled-down version of a grocery store with well-stocked shelves and coolers. Youthful shoppers pushed kid-sized carts around and made their selections. At checkout, a scanner tallied the choices according to the items' overall healthfulness and caloric value and gave each shopper a score. Junk food be damned. I walked on looking forward to bringing my grandchildren back for some fun learning.

While scouring Google Maps for potential points of interest before starting my trek, I had discovered a pin identifying "Riot Games Arena" on Olympic Boulevard in West LA. I figured I would learn what it was about when I walked by. Not so. Trees partially screened this modern low building from the street, and a small sign, easily missed by passing cars, did not clarify the nature of the business. Nobody was around.

Back home, a computer search cracked open the door on a realm entirely unknown to me—computer gaming. Readers who at least know about, if not play, the Riot Games' hit multi-player online battle video game, League of Legends, will justifiably label me a troglodyte. However, for others as clueless as I was, here is how some teens and young adults are becoming millionaires.

I reserved a seat at the Arena. It was for 1:00 p.m. on a Thursday I walked past the concession stand and the souvenir counter with over 100 twenty-somethings. I thought, "Shouldn't these people be working?" On opposite sides of the stage, two five-member teams faced each other, the 100 Thieves and the Cloud 9s. I doubt, however, that they saw much of their opponents because they were all hunched behind computer screens and wore microphones and bagel-sized headsets, with which they communicated among themselves. But no matter—the computer-generated action flashed on several large overhead video screens.

The fan sitting next to me had driven three hours that morning to witness this competition and was returning home as soon as one team prevailed. He explained that each competitor assumed the role of a "champion" out of 160 possibilities, each of whom has unique capabilities. Together the team members try to destroy their opponents' "Nexus"—home base. "Inhibitors," "turrets," "minions," and "monsters" add complexity. A game lasts about 15 minutes with each thrust, parry, and group attack called in rapid-fire narration by the announcer.

To me it was just a vibrant sound and light show, but clearly the rest of the audience was following the action and loudly voicing their approval or disdain with every advance or retreat as might spectators in an NBA championship seventh-game overtime. The League of Legends world championship apparently draws an NBA-sized following, hence the big money involved. My seatmate explained, however, that these elite gamers' reaction times slow, making them over the hill by the time they are 25 or 26. So I left after two games knowing that eventually that gamers and spectators alike would likely have to find day jobs.

I had no idea when I was planning my trek that I would get to learn about fencing. The discovery was a major "by the way." A map of West LA indicated an Amazon Center near the boundary on Olympic Boulevard. Although I had decided to limit my business visits to one-off enterprises, the prospect of peeking inside an Amazon warehouse was worth an exception. The address was near where I live, and I had driven along that section a thousand times and never recalled seeing anything as large as what I imagined an Amazon warehouse would be. How exciting—an Olympian adventure for me at Amazon.

How disappointing. At the indicated address squatted an unlabeled, windowless blue box about the size of a hardware store. I walked down the adjacent side street hoping to see a fleet of Prime trucks. Nothing.

Major dejection and rejection instantly melted away, however, when across the street I spotted a warehouse labeled LA International Fencing Center. I walked in and signed up for a lesson on another day. In the front room, there were six to eight fencing strips, which I learned later are officially known as pistes. Several of them were occupied by a student and instructor. The second room was cavernous, the size of several basketball courts. It was filled with table tennis tables, and a tournament was underway.

When I returned for my lesson, my instructor, Allex, and I had the pistes to ourselves. In the back room, table tennis competitors had morphed into girl gymnasts. Allex started with a brief history of fencing, which stems back centuries. He noted that fencing was one of only five sports that has been included in every Olympics since 1896. (The others are gymnastics, track and field, aquatics, and cycling.)

The three forms of fencing—foil, epee, and sabre—have their own histories and followers. Foil originated as a training weapon, and in modern competition, the target is just the torso when contacted with the sword's tip. Cavalrymen used sabres, and so points are now scored as if the opponents are on horseback—either with the tip or edge of the sword and from the top of the head to the hips. By contrast, epee stems from when dualists used rapiers. Today, the target, using just the tip of the weapon, is the entire body.

Not only do the swords and targets differ, so do the strategies and durations of matches. Sabre fights are action oriented and impulsive. Their aggressive attacks last only a few seconds before one fighter or the other scores a hit. By contrast, a round of epee or foil may last several minutes and appeal to those who prefer a defensive approach while waiting patiently for an opening.

Allex asked me which form I was interested in learning. "Um, er... sabre!" He showed me the basic footwork, which allows the fencer to advance or retreat quickly along the piste—dominant foot pointing forward, trailing foot turned to the side. Next I learned how to control the sabre with a loose thumb hold and flexible wrist. Then he donned a protective jacket, we both masked up, and had at it. He parried my every thrust and was kind enough not to go on the offense and stab me.

Allex told me he had students in their 70s and 80s who were winning competitions. I left with an appreciation for a sport about which I had known little. I nodded to that blue box across the street that Googe Maps had misidentified as an Amazon distribution center. The Los Angeles International Fencing Center turned out to be far more interesting.

At the next venue, the admonition was, "Don't push the pedals at the same time." With that single oral warning, we were off. Danger be damned. No telling what written warnings we had overlooked when we signed the fine-print disclaimers. Following the paperwork, my friend Phil and I pulled balaclavas over our heads and looked like bank robbers until we topped them off with motorcycle helmets. We were each directed to our individual crafts, each fitted with a bucket seat hovering two inches off the ground and four-point harnesses that secured our bodies equally close. The green flag came out and we were off. Left foot brake. Right foot "gas." Well, figurative gas because these go-karts were electric, just a humming motor providing face-flattening acceleration without any stinky exhaust fumes—perfect for an indoor raceway.

The course extended via a series of tight turns to the back of a cavernous warehouse, then up a straightaway to the finish line—around and around for 15 laps, the time of each recorded on an electronic scoreboard. Seated practically on the ground, the maximum speed of 35 miles per hour produced a sense somewhere between exhilaration and terror; and in the turns, the side-to-side forces caused the higher judgment parts of my brain to scream, "You are going to spin out. Left foot. Left foot." But, nah, more primal competitive instincts intervened. "Right foot. Right foot. Stay close to this curb and you can pass Phil on the straightaway." The race was over too soon.

The scoreboard indicated an average lap time of 28 seconds for both of us, which did not get us on the leader board. The track master said that the lap record was 21 seconds and explained that size mattered because the record holder weighed about 120 pounds.

The M2B raceway also offers private party rooms, and a darkened laser tag area spotted with large infrared obstacles to provide cover. Overall, it looked like an inviting venue for a team building event or a birthday party. Our Formula One experience came at the end of that day's ten-mile walk, and Phil gave me a ride home in airbag-equipped, late-model sedan. Not once did I have to say, "Left foot, Phil, left foot."

On another day, Phil waited with me and my personal trainer Alex, his girlfriend, and her two children, ages 21 and 15. All six of us were on time and at the right spot in front of a warehouse not far from the go-kart track. High up on the front wall, the street number stood alone. A smaller sign at eye level said No guns, no alcohol, no inebriation. Okay, okay, and okay times six people, but one problem remained. There was no entry door or sign that this was The Basement.

A few minutes after the appointed time, a vending machine embedded in the wall hinged open to allow entry into this enterprise's darkened anteroom. As our eyes adjusted to the gloom, we signed the usual all-encompassing waivers. The hostess informed us that we had entered the home of Edward Tandy, a diabolic, cannibalistic serial killer. (I wondered if there were *non-diabolic* cannibalistic killers on the loose.) I refocused and heard her say that we would soon be led into Edward's basement and locked in. Other areas of the house described on the internet were courtyard, study, and elevator shaft, which was touted as "great for date night," but still no guns or booze.

Regardless of the area reserved, Edward savored the flavor of prisoners who are incapable of finding their way to escape in 45 minutes. We received assurances that if one of us captives freaked out, it was possible to be liberated on short notice. Then we all donned hoods and were led by an unseen hand into Edward's musty, dimly lit basement apartment. Hoods off, the challenge began.

An electronic counter on the wall ticked off the seconds until Edward's planned dinner time. The hostess had previously instructed us to shout out any clues we discovered so that we could begin solving the puzzle and devise an escape. An early find was a penlight that illuminated dark corners and some Victorian-era furniture that looked like rejects from curbside recycling. We scoured shelves and drawers for keys and scrutinized walls and ceilings for scrawled messages. Time was flying.

Alex opened a cabinet and discovered that it didn't have a back in it. Being a good team player, he crawled through. Judging by his scream, I think he wished that he hadn't.

So as not to spoil the "fun" for Edward's future prisoners, I will not go into more detail, but by the fact that I am writing about the experience is evidence that we escaped. In fact, we did so with 80 seconds to spare, which our hostess said only 10 percent of prisoners achieved. Should you be tempted to thwart Edward's diabolic tendencies too, I offer this advice—include a computer-savvy teenager on your team. In our case, with keyboard-blazing fingers, he persisted and finally discovered a password that was key to our survival. On the other hand, I don't think he crawled through the cabinet with the rest of us to discover the worse-than-Halloween horrors that lay beyond.

Contrasted to the escape room, Stoney Point Park is a mecca for adventurists who favor fresh air and sunlight and like to come face to face with rocks, giant ones. These folks repeatedly press their toes and fingertips firmly against cold stone. It is, however, anything but sensual. Rather it is exhausting, possibly agonizing, even painful—at least it was for my feet when I tried it. The park is in the Chatsworth neighborhood at LA's northwest extreme. It is a stone's throw from Garden of the Gods and the Lone Ranger Rock—all huge rounded, mounded sandstone formations poking out of steeply sloped chaparral wilderness.

The prevalence and variety of these rock formations in Stoney Point Park attract human flies to their vertical surfaces. The first time I walked by, I could see a scattering of bare-headed people close to the road "bouldering" and others walking farther into the park, helmeted and carrying long coils of rope. Those who boulder can test their rock-adhering skills just a few feet off the ground. Up, left, right, and if necessary, back down far enough to jump off safely and land on a spongy pad almost as big as a twin mattress. No helmets, no ropes, but rather a couple of their bouldering buddies, male or female, standing at the edge of the pad with hands overhead, spotting and prepared to keep the falling climber from losing their balance and falling on the pad backward and possibly hitting their head.

Depending on the rock being hugged, boulderers, once reaching the top, may be able to walk or scramble down and around the backside and return to their starting point. On other rocks, however, the way down may be a reverse of the way up. One human fly told me, "Down climbing is the hardest. You can't see where to put your toes. You have to feel for it and listen to your spotters' advice." I thought, "Not sure bouldering is for me."

Several weeks later, on my way to the LA Guinea Pig Rescue, I stopped by Stoney Point, and there was not a soul in the park. It had rained the day before, and the stone huggers were all heeding the signs that said, No climbing on wet rock. Do not climb for a minimum of 72 hours after a rain. The sandstone is fragile and is very easily damaged when wet. Holds will break off.

I liked the idea of a helmet, harness, and rope to help me face the rock when it was dry, so I returned—this time for a six-hour REI class in basic rock climbing. From the back of a van the instructors supplied all eight of us climbers with harnesses, helmets, and oh-so-tight climbing shoes, which they recommended we not wear while we walked to our "classroom." This was at the base of Mozart's Wall—a 30-foot-high vertical face of sandstone, now sufficiently dry for us not to abuse it and vice versa.

Six of the students were 30-ish, one was 50-ish, and then there was me, definitely senior-ish. We first learned how to tie our harness securely onto the rope and then how to belay. Earlier that morning one of the instructors had rock hopped up the backside of Mozart's masterpiece and securely fixed carabiners there at intervals. Through these "pulleys" she had threaded the belaying rope. Now both ends of each rope were easily accessible at ground level—one for the climber's harness and the other for the belayer's hands and harness. There the rope ran through a simple but ingenious metal brake. Pull the end of the rope one way, it slides. Pull it the other way, the brake locks it tight. In this way, as the climber ascends, the belayer takes up any slack in the rope and locks it so, at worst, the climber falls only a small distance, and they can safely resume their close affection for the rock.

The instructors stressed safety and close communication between the climber and the belayer. We learned to check each other's harness adjustments before confirming readiness. Climber: "Belay on?" Belayer when ready: "Belay on." Climber: "Climbing." Belayer: "Climb on."

And up we went—well, sort of. The instructors started us on a pitch that was about 75 degrees off horizontal, so it was similar to climbing a very steep roof—but here we were looking for the next quarter- to half-inch-wide ledge or pocket to stick a foot against or grasp with several fingers. Push up with one foot or pull up with one hand and search for the next possible irregularity in the rock, all the time receiving encouragement from below. After a couple of runs for each of us up the bunny slope, we progressed to Mozart's best, but there was more gasping than harmonious music.

I was the least skillful of the bunch. That was no surprise, because when I get out of bed every morning, I rediscover how inflexible a senior-ish, rather fit, person can be. For instance, the others were making moves that brought their knee up to touch their shoulder before pasting their foot to the rock and shooting themselves upward by straightening their hip and knee. I remembered last doing that climbing trees in grade school.

Nonetheless, the course was engaging, and I consoled myself with anticipated future successes in more grounded sports. I liked the sentiment expressed when the belayer would say, "Climb on." I decided to adopt that encouraging green flag message for other activities. I now say to myself, "Walk on."

Which of these aforementioned amusements did I like the best? Discovery Cube was fun, but one visit was sufficient. Despite the stunning sound and light extravaganza of League of Legends, watching Gen Zs nicknamed Twisted Fate, Nendoroid Ashe, and Blitzcrank perform electronic battle was far too sedentary, even if it might eventually be comprehensible. Also in semi-darkness and requiring a specific venue, the escape room was intentionally incomprehensible, at least at first. Rock climbing and go-karting require rocks and a track, respectively, and so are also restricted to specific locations. Fencing isn't much fun without an opponent, whereas a punching bag substitutes for one in boxing, and I can shadowbox and do planks and pushups anywhere on any day. Plus, the boxing lesson was a good total-body workout. I felt refreshed. Isn't that what fun should be about? Ideally, work should be fun too.

CHAPTER 12

WORK

With over 3 million people surrounded by LA's city line, you can expect a typical metropolitan mix of bankers, gardeners, lawyers, construction workers, health care professionals, teachers, software engineers, homemakers, students, and on and on. Of course, the entertainment industry stands tall and attracts myriad screen writers, actors, camera operators, editors, and so forth. But around the city limits, I ran into a vanishingly small number of people embracing conventional occupations.

Were they just inside when I walked by? Maybe their businesses were without signage and therefore unrecognized? Perhaps these businesses gravitated to central areas such as downtown and Century City, far away from my path along the border. Or maybe they had been repelled by Los Angeles and were conducting business in surrounding areas.

For the purpose of my trek, I was happy that there was space near the city's boundaries for small businesses, often unique, and rarely glamorous or well-known. Here are some that I found most fascinating. I divide them into services and goods.

It was in Sun Valley that I took my boxing lesson. It is a neighborhood on the northern border of Los Angeles, and like other neighborhoods in the area, is zoned for agriculture. A lot of residents keep horses on ranchettes out there on the border of civilization. I describe the Kindred Spirits Care Farm, Wildlife Learning Center, and Love Always Sanctuary in Chapter 5 (Nurture), and they are all within a few miles of each other. The area is animal friendly, especially for some lucky dogs.

The sign at the entrance of Paradise Ranch hints at what fun is in store behind the gates. "CAGE-FREE PET RESORT, PLUS WATER PARK FOR DOGS." I didn't have time to visit the day I walked by, and when I called to arrange for a visit, I was told to bring my dog along for an evaluation. Weeks later, Jazzy, our six-pound bundle of loving fluff, and I returned. After filling out some forms regarding vaccinations, temperament, and habits (for Jazzy, not me), I handed her to a staff member, who asked me to come back in 30 to 45 minutes. I ran an errand and returned to learn that Jazzy had received a favorable assessment, and I was invited to bring her back for boarding or day care whenever I wanted. I was as elated as one might feel if one's child had just gained admission to an elite school.

Based on my brief tour, I think any dog would have a fun time there. The other dogs certainly seemed happy. The guest list averages 100 and swells to 140 at holiday time. To manage their clientele, Paradise Ranch has multiple large, play areas, each with a mix of pavement, artificial grass, palm-tree shade, and sun. Hibiscus shrubs add some color. Several areas have pools. One is shallow for wading. One is deep for large-dog jumping and swimming.

Dogs, segregated roughly by size, were everywhere, roaming around in packs within each enclosure, snoozing in a thatched cabana, or sunning themselves on low cots. A staff member is continuously present with each group and early on establishes themself at the top of the social order so that the guests will behave. In order to maintain alpha-dog status, the staff do not play much with their canine guests.

The dogs rotate from one play area to another every several hours to avoid boredom. In the evening, an attendant takes the dogs inside one of several well-kept, single-story Mediterranean-style houses on the property, and the dogs decide for themselves on which bed and with which pals to settle for the night. They are taken out at about 9:00

p.m. and again at about 11:00 p.m. for potty breaks. An attendant stays in the same area of the house all night.

I remarked about the TV on the wall. My guide said that it was for the dogs and was turned on if there were disturbing noises such as fireworks or thunder in the area, but no late-night talk shows. It can be really hot in Sun Valley, and as you might expect by now, the house is air conditioned. In the morning, the bedding gets changed and the dogs get weighed. Even though they have their own food, it is common that they may lose a little weight because they are so active, and they may be worn out for several days when they get home. I would have only one problem with Jazzy staying at Paradise Ranch. Would it be fair that she had more fun on vacation than I did?

If you like parrots, you might like a "by the way" business I discovered that can cater to your needs for avian acquisition, accoutrements, and advice. Parrots Naturally is a storefront shop in the Woodland Hills area of the San Fernando Valley. In addition to a wide selection of birds for sale, the store is filled with cages and toys of all shapes and sizes, feeders, food, and everything else a feathered pet might need. The owners, husband and wife, breed and raise the birds they sell. New owners agree to let Parrots Naturally know if they have to give up the bird for any reason, including outliving their owner, which is conceivable since some parrots live 80 years.

Rather than a dog or parrot, maybe you need a place to temporarily "board" a work of art, your massive baseball card collection, or some cases of fine wine. I found a good place. As I walked along, it was another "by the way" surprise, revealed by a sign across the top of a one-story warehouse behind a driveway gate in West LA. The attendant who buzzed me in to the Los Angeles Fine Arts and Wine Storage Company showed me around. "Art" can be defined not only paintings, but also books, costumes, you name it.

The standard art lockers are four feet wide, ten feet deep, and eight feet tall with plywood walls and open tops. This allows for good air circulation and keeps the temperature at 70 degrees F and the relative humidity at 55%. In a separate area, the wine lockers are maintained at 55 degrees F. The standard lockers will hold 20 cases and are priced according to how far up the wall they are. Those at ground level are more expensive than the ones four or five tiers up. Rolling stairways are provided, best used when entirely sober. For avid collectors, they also have lockers capable of storing 500 cases (6000 bottles). Before committing to taking one of your cases home to enjoy, there is an on-site tasting room. Packing, transportation, and installation services are also available.

As I walked away, I wondered about transporting 500 cases of wine, which would require a big truck and a competent driver. That reminded me of the day I got kicked out of the Sunshine Canyon Landfill (details later) and the sour frame of mind that followed.

My mood began to improve a mile down the road when I happened across a large parking area in the middle of nowhere with several signs visible from afar: GSF Truck Training. I thought, *"Maybe I'll get my commercial driver's license and go back to the landfill in my own big rig."* I met Sergio, who told me what would be involved. GSF offers a six-week course, 30 hours per week, that teaches everything from inspecting the truck to managing the 10-speed manual transmission and backing up. GSF keeps a delivery truck and a big rig parked at the Department of Motor Vehicles, so students do not have to bring their own on test day. Graduates can earn $120,000 to $150,000 per year. They usually start as over-the-road drivers and with seniority can drive locally and regularly sleep at home.

I told him that I had heard that truck drivers are often fatigued and so it was a good idea to stay as far away as possible from 18-wheelers on the freeway. He confirmed that these land cruisers are not highly maneuverable and take far longer to stop than passenger vehicles, so it is best to give them wide clearance. Regarding fatigue, he said the newer trucks have monitors that track the vehicle's time and location and limit driving time to ten hours. Then with a two-hour break, the driver can go for two more.

I wondered out loud if self-driving trucks were going to put drivers and GSF out of business. Sergio shrugged his shoulders.

Having overcome my landfill distress, I walked on, informed, and happy with my present mode of transportation.

Those were some of the unique services that I encountered. What about interesting goods for sale or rent?

A half-mile stretch of Chandler Boulevard in North Hollywood is remarkable for several reasons. It is named for Harry Chandler, who in the late 1800s started a company to deliver morning newspapers, which eventually led to him becoming general manager of the Los Angeles Times, marrying the publisher's daughter, and taking over the newspaper's reins on the death of his father-in-law. Chandler transformed it into the leading newspaper in the West and unashamedly used its columns to promote Los Angeles in general and particularly his own extensive business interests. These included oil, banking, shipping, and especially real estate development. For a while he was the largest private landowner in the US.

Chandler Boulevard is unusually wide. In its time, it accommodated a railroad line alongside. The right of way is now a nicely landscaped ribbon park with sculptures, a play area, and exercise equipment spaced at intervals along a bike and pedestrian path. Low-rise and mostly windowless warehouses provide a background for the park and a "canvas" for mural artists.

I walked almost to the end of the half-mile-long string of murals and could see one last warehouse ahead with an unembellished blue wall. I thought, *How boring. Turn around, Roy, and continue the trek.* I then recalled my poor decision to let Ms. Frowny intimidate me at the Department of Water and Power. *Remember, slow down, take it all in. It's the journey, not the destination.* I decided to walk close enough to see what the building contained.

I am glad I did. It introduced me to the amazing realm of prop houses, which, I was soon to learn, pepper North Hollywood and the nearby cluster of movie and TV studios.

Two workers in the Almost Christmas Prop Shop welcomed me in. "Sure, have a look around." The cavernous building was packed with every imaginable Christmas decoration—soldier nutcrackers six inches to six feet tall, completely decorated Christmas trees even taller, sleighs, full-sized gingerbread houses, lawn ornaments, lights, garlands, nativity scenes. I asked one of the workers, who was unpacking a large box of five-inch silver balls, "Do you decorate much at home for Christmas?" "Not so much, I pretty much get my fix here."

Within a five or six block area of Almost Christmas, other prop shops have their unique specializations. For instance, the Costume Rental Corporation specializes in military and police uniforms. They outfitted all the actors for *Saving Private Ryan*. "How many uniforms do you have?" "Oh, millions, come take a peek." Lisa walked me into the warehouse, which could have easily contained a football field. I looked down the aisle and counted at least sixty racks, each with four bars of tightly packed clothes. "There are more in the next room. We also have a badge shop on site to replicate any insignia to make our uniforms historically correct." She said it was fun to see movies, TV shows, and advertisements where the actors were wearing costumes she had managed.

I next stopped at The Ruby Fashion Library, which provides mainly contemporary clothes for the entertainment industry. Jena said that designers make clothing, which stylists assemble into outfits and place on consignment. I used their restroom before moving on. Stenciled on the wall was, Give a girl the right shoes and she can conquer the world. Marilyn Monroe. My scuffed walking shoes seemed pedestrian as I ambled on.

Undoubtedly the most fascinating prop shop I visited was History for Hire. Two aging rickshaws flanked the entry, which opened into a claustrophobic cave of memorabilia far more diverse and numerous than any flea market or antique store I had ever visited. Does the script call for a 1950s grocery store aisle with cleaning supplies such as Deft, Salvo, Ajax, Vel, and Lux? No problem. The head-high shelves were full. Need a 1909 catcher's mitt and mask? Sure. How about a typewriter or telephone of the correct vintage? Take your pick from hundreds. Same for trunks and suitcases.

I asked Joelene if all this "stuff" weighed on her. "Oh no, I love going to flea markets, and I just finished restoring my grandfather's 1912 typewriter."

She asked me if I knew why this area was so prop-house dense. "No." "During World War II, these warehouses were all aircraft assembly plants, which were conveniently located next to Burbank Airport. The whole area was camouflaged to look like farms and suburban neighborhoods. After the war, the aircraft companies moved out, which provided plenty of space for prop houses supplying the rapidly growing entertainment industry."

Joelene also told me that there were other prop houses in the area that specialized in medical equipment and sporting goods. Later I checked the map. Alas, they are out of bounds for this trek, maybe for my next one.

Walking east from downtown LA, low warehouses, several schools, and an art gallery spread out along 7th Street. At the corner of Santa Fe Avenue, a stately five-story brick and glass building is marked with an artfully designed but easily overlooked "W." Now occupied by the Warner Musical Group, this building opened in 1914 when 1,100 workers began assembling 300 Model T Fords a day. Although the building is on the National Register of Historic Places, the only visible nod to its industrial beginnings is a glass case in the entryway. It displays several pieces of heavy industrial equipment disassembled when the factory closed in 1929.

En route to another historical landmark a mile farther south and east, on Google Maps I spotted "Poison Ivy," which drew my curiosity. To get there I had to turn into a wide alley rather than walking down the street another half block, which was the most direct route to my next known point of interest. Poison Ivy was out of business. In my curious pursuit, however, I turned up two "by the ways," which are always fun.

The first was another cavernous warehouse with a sandwich board out front, TRIM 4 LESS. The owner was at the front counter. "Sure, look around." Shelving 16 to 20 feet high was stuffed full of cardboard cartons. In some instances, a sample of the box's contents and quantity was taped on the outside: buttons, zippers, buckles, pendants, cording, small plastic rings, stretch lace, and rickrack (whatever that is). Packing in one more button would have made the place explode.

The owner, a middle-aged man, said that his grandfather had started the business, that they got most of their inventory from overruns from large clothing manufacturers, and that his clients are mostly smaller, local garment shops. He said that Trim 4 Less had the largest collection of buttons in the US. I asked him if he dreamed about buttons. "Yes, in my younger days." I also asked him if he was preparing his kids to take over. "No, one is a dentist, the other is a psychologist. They are interested in the property, but that's all."

Farther down the alley on the other side, I saw a pickup truck with a towering stack of tied-down corrugated cardboard pull into a courtyard. I followed it in, where an end loader was pushing mountains of flattened boxes away from the gateway so that other trucks, several with large roll-off bins, could enter. Again, an on-site owner welcomed my questions.

Angelus Western Paper Fibers collects, sorts, and distributes waste cardboard and white paper—the offcuts from large printing projects. The company supplies clients like Nordstroms and Macy's with dumpsters, which AWPF exchanges periodically. The trucks are weighed on entry and exit. Small-time operators, like the man in the pickup truck, may make several runs and earn a couple hundred dollars a day. For two shifts, five and a half days a week, the paper and cardboard are sorted, compressed, baled, and shipped to paper mills, mostly in Asia, some in the US It made me consider starting to break down and stack all of the Amazon boxes that arrive at home, but presently I put them in the blue barrel and hope they make their way to some facility like AWPF.

I then exited the alley and walked to an iconic but shuttered giant that I had previously identified and which I could easily see from six or eight blocks away. It is a nine-story-high Art Deco tower with large letters across the top identifying it as Sears. The building looms over the one- and two-story buildings in this mostly industrial area. When it opened in 1927, it was one of the largest buildings in LA and was one of Sears's nine regional mail order and distribution centers. A retail outlet occupied the ground floor. At a time when Amazon was just the name of a long river, this building was a technological marvel. Employees on roller skates picked up items that had been ordered and dropped them on corkscrew slides, which sent them on their way by truck or train to happy catalog buyers. Time flies.

Along the way, I found an array of other businesses, all far smaller than Sears, that sold goods. I will mention some of the most memorable ones in the general sequence that I encountered them, starting at LA's northern border and walking my way around the boundary counterclockwise.

Tucked in beside the Foothill Freeway, a greenhouse the size of two basketball courts is home to LA Succulents. Midcareer, the owner turned his back on marketing and converted his hobby into a thriving business of propagating and selling cacti and succulents. Along the line he learned that he cannot ship to anywhere outside the southwestern US in the wintertime because his plants do not tolerate cold. He said that I should come back in the summer when many of the plants would be blooming. That would be a sight indeed, because even without blooms, the symmetry and variation among these slow-growing gems was amazing. It was a good lesson in botany. I asked his assistant how many of these plants he had at home and if he knew their Latin names. "Sixty five. Yes."

Not far away, California Firewood Sales has ricks of wood (citrus, almond, eucalyptus, white and red oak, olive, and English walnut) the size of small houses. I found it remarkable to learn that these gargantuan stacks nearly disappeared during lockdown. Everybody was at home barbecuing.

I asked the clerk at Record Surplus in West Los Angeles how many records he had at home. "Five or six thousand long play albums." There were far more in the store, and it made me feel nostalgic to see the covers of records from my formative years—The Kingston Trio; Peter, Paul, and Mary; Bob Dylan. (You will reveal your age if you admit to staring at the album cover while listening to the music.)

Walking on to Venice, where everything is a bit wonky and free-range, Meshika the Hatmaker, in his behind-the-house studio, did not disappoint. Also known as Alberto, he is the third generation in his family to make hats, mostly brimmed, both ready to wear and custom-sized and shaped. The creativity he employs in these works of art is impressive, and wearing any one of his hats would gain the attention and approving nods of passersby. Some look like they have survived a stampede. He distresses others by setting them on fire or scuffing them with sandpaper. The prime ones may sport a Superman pin, feather, or playing card to complete their statement. I felt a bit shabby leaving in my baseball cap labeled Los Angeles, but that was my persona for the trek.

At the top of the Shoestring in a neighborhood called Harbor City, I happened onto a mulch yard. To stop in, I definitely would have been overdressed in a Meshika hat. Two good ole boys were sitting in lawn chairs by the gate, in the shade of a yellow end loader. The owner said that he used to get dirt from swimming pool projects, but not so much anymore—now it comes from retaining wall and building site excavations. He mixes the soil with wood chips but does not add garden trimmings. "Too many contaminants." He sells the mulch mostly to landscapers for groundcover.

He put the area into historical perspective. "Harbor City? Hell, we are over two miles from navigable water in San Pedro, but somebody wanted to dredge a canal and make this area the port. He didn't get beyond naming it. Now I'm sitting here high and dry, selling mulch."

It was at least 20 miles farther along before I became aware of my next business attraction. My nose knew first—chili pepper in the air. This was the home of Tampico Spice in South LA. I met David, who said that his grandfather started the business in 1947 by buying $35 worth of spices, packaging them in small cellophane envelopes, and selling them to corner markets across the Southland. He more than doubled his money, which he used to buy more spices. Now David oversees this international enterprise that buys spices and herbs from around the world and tests them for contaminants. If present, he rejects the giant bags and sends them back. If pure, the spices and herbs are ground, packaged, and delivered to grocery stores, restaurants, and industrial food kitchens. During my tour of the warehouse, forklifts were zipping back and forth taking waist-high cardboard drums to the loading dock: Hot Taco Mix 150 lbs, Pumpkin Pie Spice 200 lbs, and Steak Seasoning, 250 lbs. Nothing bland about this inventory.

Eight miles north and east took me to an industrial area near downtown and home to a real Amazon distribution center, a metal powder coating facility, several snarling guard dogs, a noisy aluminum/glass/  plastic recycling center, and a railroad-right-of-way cleaning contractor. Many more businesses were identified by names posted on their gates or buildings but without any indication the business they were conducting. Two, however, stood out, and they could not possibly have been more different from one another.

The sign on the warehouse wall indicated SANDLER BROTHERS WIPING RAGS. A towel was drawn hanging over the period. They take fabric remnants from the nearby garment district along with old clothes and linens, remove any buttons and zippers, sort them by texture and color, cut them to standard sizes, bundle them in 10- to 50-pound packs, and sell them to anybody who wipes—car shops, factories, institutions. The textures in white include sheeting, thermal blankets, sweats, tablecloths, and napkins. Those same textures along with denim, corduroy, and flannel also come in colors. Their tagline on their website is, "It's lonely at the top, but it's clean."

On the next street, a low warehouse was signed ABC CASKETS in large letters, Factory in small letters and OPEN TO THE PUBLIC in medium ones. I wasn't sure whether it was the caskets or the factory that was open, so I headed in. Joey, another third-generation business owner, met me in their showroom and walked me around. When I told him I was sticking as close as possible to the city-limit line, he said, "Follow me." He walked me down a back hall, opened a door onto an alley, and pointed to the pavement. I thought he was kicking me out. "That's the city line." After confirming that ABC was "in bounds," he showed me their extensive woodworking shop where they make caskets from scratch in a variety of woods, the spray booth for either painting or varnishing them, and the sewing area where the interiors are completed.

From afar I saw Joey's son talking to a customer, proving that ABC is morphing into a fourth-generation family business. I asked Joey what he planned to do in retirement, and we shared our interest in the architecture of old homes. He showed me his floor-to-ceiling cabinet filled with books on architecture. I will describe some of those homes in the next chapter, but by then, it was time for lunch.

Just as white-collar businesses are not magnetically attracted to the boundary line, neither are upscale eateries that would cater to them. For several reasons that's fine with me. I like good food, but I am neither a foodie nor a wine connoisseur. (My appreciation of fermented grapes stops at being able to distinguish white from red, so I have not rented a locker at LA Fine Arts and Wine Storage.) Secondly, on my trek I wanted a quick lunch. Tablecloths, table service, and menus in French were out. Also, I feared hostess rejection if she disapproved of my baseball cap, daypack, and trekking poles. Rather I stuck to counter service, and even in some instances, window service. Nonetheless, I had interesting experiences and enjoyed tasty food. To organize my descriptions in some logical order, I compare my dining experiences to rungs on a ladder. I will start about a third of the way up (counter service and indoor seating) and work my way down.

I love a good cheeseburger, and fortuitously, two of the places consistently ranking high on several lists of "best cheeseburgers in LA" were in my strike zone. One is in the Eagle Rock neighborhood in the northeast corner of Los Angeles. It was March when I walked past this second Eagle Rock on my adventure and conveniently found myself at the Oinkster at lunchtime. At the counter, an Oink poster promoted their St. Patrick's Dad Burger. This was pictured at about seven inches tall with a potato bun housing "grade A Nebraska ground beef, sliced corned beef, Oinkster mustard, pickles, and bubbles 'n squeak." (I learned that the latter is a mix of shredded potatoes and cabbage fried together). I considered the Dad Burger to be an outrageous affront for a middle-of-the-day party of one, so I opted for a traditional cheeseburger, which was delicious. Could this be topped?

Hawkins House of Burgers is a cherished institution in Watts. This neighborhood is in the southeast section of LA, not far from where the Shoestring takes off toward Wilmington and San Pedro. Whereas The Oinkster has counter service, HH has two windows ten feet apart, one for ordering. The other opens periodically when a number is announced, and a white paper bag is handed through. The menu lists "The Leaning Tower of Watts." Its picture dwarfs the Oinkster's Dad Burger in height several times over. It includes three half pound patties, hot link, pastrami, eggs, and bacon. It comes with "large fry" and two

medium drinks. I let common sense prevail and ordered an ordinary cheeseburger and peach cobbler. Both were delectable. I would have to go back and forth between The Oinkster and HH several times on the same day to determine if one cheeseburger was better than the other, but the two classics are 20 miles apart. That would be a lot of walking.

I encountered peach cobbler on several other days, and that always made me happy. Crustees (previously described in Chapter 9), Granny's Kitchen (Southern style soul food), and Big Momma's Bayou Shack (New Orleans fare) form a triangle about five miles on an edge in South LA. In other words, one could theoretically eat at all three of these counter-serve, sit-down-inside restaurants at the beginning, middle, and end of a ten-mile walk. To do so, however, I would recommend ambulance backup.

Big Momma served me gumbo, which was filled with so much crab, shrimp, andouille sausage, chicken, and vegetables that my spoon stood up straight in the middle of the bowl between bites, even when the gumbo was half gone. Other offerings that I would like to try sometime are her shrimp po'boy, brisket, barbequed ribs, and boudin balls, which are shrimp, crabmeat, and rice rolled together and deep fried.

Menu items at Granny's Kitchen are found more widely across the South than just New Orleans, but to my knowledge, not in LA. Just perusing the menu was filling. Highlights included neck bones, pig feet, chicken and waffles, catfish nuggets, greens, and black-eyed peas. I wasn't feeling adventuresome that day because I knew I still had miles to walk, so I settled on baked chicken, greens, and mac-and-cheese. The peach cobbler was not yet out of the oven, so I had more cornbread for dessert. It was cooked in a skillet like a pancake. Oven-baked cornbread loses freshness the longer the cornbread remains in the pan. Pan-cooked cornbread arrives hot off the stove for each diner.

Every culture seems to have its own version of Southern cornbread to use as a wrap, pusher, or sopper. Think pita, bagel, crepe, taco. Along Foothill Boulevard in Sylmar, I discovered another wrap. This is horse country, so the diner's name, Ranch Side Café, did not surprise me, but smaller lettering did. American Mexican Ethiopian. It was midmorning, but I had to try it.

The owner was at the counter. She and her sister had immigrated from Ethiopia 25 years earlier and started the restaurant serving Mexican and American fare. Patrons asked about adding Ethiopian food with its traditional spices, and so they did. I ordered the Ethiopian vegetarian plate with injera. She pronounced it "in-JER-ah." The veggies (cabbage, beets, peas, collard greens, red lentils, and chickpeas) were arranged artfully on a plate-sized round of injera flatbread. It is made from a grain called teff, which is naturally gluten free. Before walking on, I read about teff on my cell phone. The Ethiopians use it not only for injera, but also for porridge, alcoholic drinks, baby food, animal feed, and when mixed with mud, construction material. Good stuff.

Stepping down one rung on the ladder of dining ambiance are establishments with counter service and only outdoor seating. I walked past this "restaurant" midafternoon about eight miles into a planned 11-mile segment. The gate to the church parking lot on which Pinoy Big Mouth was sited was locked. I could see at the far end several white canopy tents that were tightly secured. No one was around. How strange. I had invited Phil (go-kart competitor and escape room companion) and his wife Amy, both ardent foodies, to join me there for dinner and to give me a ride home from this Wilmington location when we were finished. But now, two hours before the internet-indicated opening time of 5:00 PM, prospects for having some Filipino (aka Pinoy) food were questionable.

I continued walking to finish that day's segment and got back to the gate at 4:45. People were stirring. Great. The walls on the canopy tents were rolled up, several long rectangular charcoal grills on the parking lot were aflame, and a ragtag assortment of folding tables and lawn chairs had appeared on the adjacent lawn. Phil and Amy arrived. At 5:00, the gate rolled open. Game on!

The proprietor immediately recognized us as non-Pinoy. "Have you been here before?" "No." "Let me show you around." On a table under the canopy, shoebox-sized stainless-steel containers sat on beds of ice. One by one, he lifted the lids to reveal bamboo skewers supporting chunks of … Before I could begin forming a description of them, he said, "You have to understand, Filipinos love these choices: marinated pig ear, and here, marinated pig snout."

In the next container were long, white stringy somethings skewered back and forth making them look like a twisty mountain road. "Chicken intestines." "Oh." "The skewers are $1.50 each. Select what you want and bring them to the checkout where you can also get baked chicken, rice, and drinks. Then you grill the skewers yourself. There are containers of Pinoy barbecue sauce and brushes next to the grills."

Within a short time, other diners, all of Filipino heritage, joined us at the grills and advised us on the fine points of grilling and sauce application. Conversations around the grills and tables were lively, and several groups of four to eight were clearly enjoying one another's company. I watched them for any signs of gastronomic distress. None were apparent. Amy, Phil, and I were more contemplative as we de-skewered our morsels and sampled them. "Chewy." "A little fatty." "The sauce is good." "It definitely does not taste like chicken." Overall, I would rate the experience as more of a catalyst for socialization than a meal.

The next to lowest rung on the ladder of fine dining is window service with, at most, outdoor seating. (The very lowest rung, which I avoided, is standing in a 7-Eleven eating a bag of pretzels.) Here are three "second rung" eateries that I visited.

Chorizo is a pork link sausage that originated in Spain and Portugal and found its way with regional variations into many national cuisines in Spanish- and Portuguese-speaking countries. For Mexican food, chili pepper and vinegar are usually mixed with the ground meat. Chorizo is the central ingredient in the fare served through a window at Chori-man in San Pedro. Humberto is a fourth-generation artisan chorizo maker who started in 2013. At first, he pulled his sausages in a rolling cooler door-to-door and sold about a pound a day. Now established, he grinds 52,000 pounds of meat a year, which works out to almost 150 pounds a day. I asked his wife what their best seller was, and so I ordered The Chori-Man Breakfast Burrito that had maple-habanero chorizo, crispy potatoes, two runny eggs, and cheese. I sat on a nearby bus bench and indulged.

X'tiosu is a window-serve eatery located in Boyle Heights, east of downtown LA. To pronounce its name, which means "thank you" in Zapotec, start with "sh" and the rest follows phonetically, *shtee-OH-soo*. From a rural village in Oaxaca, Mexico, two brothers immigrated to LA as teenagers and had to learn Spanish on arrival, because Zapotec was their native language. After working in a Lebanese restaurant for a while, they opened X'tiosu and offer Mexican-Lebanese fusion dishes.

A mother and her young son were waiting for their order when she saw Tammie and me baffled by the menu. "This is your first time, right?" "Yep." "Get the chicken shawarma tacos. You won't be disappointed." We did and we weren't. I also had Oaxacan humus, which the brothers, X'tiosu's sole employees, make from Mexican black beans. It tasted good but had a faint lavender hue, which I did not find appetizing. So I closed my eyes.

Also in Boyle Heights is Tacos Y Birria La Unica, a food truck ranked among the 15 best in LA. It parks curbside at the same spot six days a week, raises its side awning, and sets out folding tables and chairs on the sidewalk. Its name means Unique Tacos and Stewed Meat. Unique indeed. I asked several patrons in line what they recommended, and they all responded, "Get the shredded goat taco." So I did along with two more crispy tacos, one topped with braised beef lip, the other with beef tongue. No problem telling one from the other. Condiment toppings included chopped onion, cilantro, radish slices, and a splash of "mild" salsa verde, I liked the shredded goat the best, then the tongue, and then the lip (fatty). The menu also listed beef "cabeza." I wasn't certain what part of the head that might be and decided that a two-course lunch was enough, so I walked on.

I came across three stores, all of them in corner shopping centers, that sold drinking water. Treated on site, purified water usually sold for $.50 a gallon, and alkali (minerals added) for $1.50. Each enterprise had impressive stainless-steel tanks topped with gauges. Tubes snaked everywhere, and faucets placed all in a row were ready for customers to fill their own containers. I asked myself how serious two of the shops were about promoting health. On one's façade, Liquor was in the largest lettering followed by progressively smaller signs indicating Free 2-liter Coca Cola with 750 ml purchase, then Water Store, and finally tiny letters explaining that the 750 ml purchase referred to liquor, not water.

On the counter in the other store, Slim Jims, Reese's Miniature Cups, and Bubbaloos were beckoning for impulse purchase.

Water Village in the Eagle Rock neighborhood was a pleasant contrast. The whole place was clean and neat. Its tanks were the largest, visible through a large glass window at the back of the store. No other consumables, liquid or solid, were available—just water and an array of containers for transporting and storing it. Their water tasted fine but not discernably different from city water at home, where it costs less than a penny a gallon. I have been drinking it for decades without apparent ill effect, so I wished the proprietor luck and walked on.

CHAPTER 13

ART

When I was five, my parents drove my grandparents, my two siblings, and me 1,700 miles from our home in Kansas City to Mexico City for a vacation. It was entirely out of character for my middle-class Midwestern parents. (We normally vacationed every summer at a rustic cabin in Colorado.) I wish my parents were around now so that I could ask them what the hell prompted them to make such an out-of-the-ordinary trip.

Two things I remember about Mexico City—the aggressive shoeshine boys my age and the Diego Rivera murals that depicted Mexican history, with which I had no connection. I did not understand the murals but could sense that they were epic. Actually, I'm not sure if I remember the murals themselves or the postcards we brought home, but I do recall that the murals were in porticos and entirely protected from the weather.

Then throughout my growing-up years in the Midwest, I came face to face many times with the murals painted by regional artist Thomas Hart Benton. They were all *inside* public spaces. Come to think of it, so is da Vinci's *Last Supper*, and locally, the same is true for Dean Cornwell's depiction of early California history inside the rotunda of the Los Angeles Public Library Central Branch.

What a surprise then, to walk around LA and see murals painted on *outside* walls. I came across a number of them on my trek, none by muralists as famous as those mentioned, at least not yet, but nonetheless accomplished artists intent on making statements, recording history, or just amusing the viewer or themselves.

I learned that Los Angeles has a long tradition of outside murals dating back almost 100 years. It is entirely disputable which city should be called the mural capital of the world because works come and go and people may disagree about what differentiates murals from advertisements and graffiti, but LA ranks high by any standard. The City's ranking in the pantheon of public art took a dive in the 1980s when it was beleaguered with billboard blight, and officials tried to restrict this form of public advertising. Some advertisers presented their outdoor promotions as murals rather than as commercials and claimed that their free-speech rights were being abridged. These claims were disputed in courts for years, during which time the moratorium on public art was strict.

In 2013 Los Angeles amended its municipal code to allow preservation of existing non-commercial murals and to permit creation of new ones. The ordinance defined a mural as a "one-of-a-kind, hand-painted, hand-tiled, or digitally printed image on the exterior wall of a building that does not contain any commercial message." It cannot be more than 100 feet high or have flashing lights or moving parts. With these stipulations and clarifications, mural art has thrived, more in some sections of LA than others.

Along the course of my trek, I found maximum mural mania in Venice, where any flat surface, especially if it was an alley-facing wall, was likely hosting a painting. Themes in Venice are as eclectic as its free-spirited residents—for instance, a scowling monster reaching out to sink its claws in unsuspecting boardwalk strollers, floral designs of great intricacy, and the Luminaries of Pantheism. This magnum opus covers the entire 75-foot-long side of a two-story building, which is the headquarters for the Paradise Project, "dedicated to celebrating and connecting diverse independent free thinkers who are deeply spiritual about science and nature." The mural includes 16 portraits of a rather diverse group of individuals ranging from Lao Tzu to Henry David Thoreau, Carl Sagan, Emily Dickinson, and Nikola Tesla. Einstein, Spinoza, and Jung are also depicted, minus major portions of their foreheads taken up by the building's square second-story windows.

Sometimes artists incorporate the building's elements into their mural, turning blemishes into features. My favorite is a mural with a woman holding what appears to be a large cue card (the wall's sole second-story window). An umbrella-shaped awning over the entry door immediately below doubles as her skirt. This painting is part of another mural-dense area, which is along Van Nuys Boulevard in Pacoima, hugging LA's northern border. Here "Mural Mile" stretches for two miles and is home to 35 paintings that are helping rehabilitate what used to be a rather seedy and undesirable strip of shops peddling various vices.

One of the newest murals, 300 feet long and three stories high, resonated particularly with me because it depicts Zeus, the blind owl that I had met previously at the Wildlife Learning and Conservation Center. "Hi Zeus. You're famous." This mural and many of the others nearby reflect the culture of the community and serve as a source of neighborhood pride.

Retaining walls may be the best "canvas" for outdoor muralists because these surfaces are unblemished by windows and doors and may extend horizontally seemingly forever. For instance, The Great Wall of Los Angeles extends for over a half mile along the Tujunga Wash flood control channel in the middle of the San Fernando Valley. Its location was too far inside the LA city limits for me to walk along and describe the mural in detail, but the presence of an adjacent bike path and park make the Great Wall an attraction for urban explorers not hewing closely to the city limits, at least when storm water is not racing to the ocean.

My favorite retaining-wall mural is on Los Liones Drive, a stone's throw across Sunset Boulevard from the Self-Realization Shrine and up the hill just a bit from Pacific Coast Highway. The nearly hundred-yard stretch depicts a Southern California wilderness and a small stream with eye-to-eye views of artfully rendered scrub jays, California quail with their novel forward-drooping head plumes, owls, squirrels, rabbits, and a couple of mountain lions and a rattlesnake on the prowl. I had just completed the last wilderness segment of my adventure when I walked along, happy to see renditions of some of the animals I had encountered, relieved that I had not seen several of the others up this close.

Having walked by numerous examples of mural and graffiti art, I was inspired to paint a wall myself. Where would this be possible to do without getting arrested? Venice, of course. On the beach are two four-foot-high walls with a combined length of perhaps 100 feet. Nearby is a 20-foot-tall cone-shaped structure, concrete picnic tables, and a scattering of trashcans. These are "easels" for the Venice Art Walls project, where on weekends artists are encouraged to express their creativity (and maybe keep their masterpieces off billboards, overpasses, and freeway sound walls).

Several artists were at work when I arrived, and I asked where I could set up shop. "Anywhere you want." "But that means I will have to paint over what's already here." "No problem. It eventually happens to all of us." That fellow, in his 20s, spoke with a bit of an accent. I asked him where he was from. "Poland. I am in the US for the first time." His girlfriend and he had spent the previous week in San Francisco, and now they were staying in a rental in Venice. "We head home in two days." He had learned from the internet that he could paint a wall in Venice, and that was how he was spending half a day. Not for every first-time tourist, but hey, this is the magnetism of Venice.

With dark spray paint, I covered over a nice floral design and then used masking tape to shape the outline of LA's city limits. I filled it in with turquoise, labeled it WALKING THE LINE, and had a passerby take a picture of me and my rather crude creation compared to the adjacent artistry. I gathered my supplies, walked over to the boardwalk to get something to eat, and had the idea that I should also include the URL for my website, lacitylimits.info, on my magnum opus. I was back there in under 20 minutes only to find that somebody had already commandeered my tract and applied their base coat. So much for my future as a muralist.

There is another "canvas" for mural art that is sized and situated such that it does not require a cherry picker, scaffold, or ladder to paint. Every intersection in LA that has a stop light also has a small-refrigerator-sized utility box perched on the corner. Inside are the electronics that orchestrate the intersectional light show—greens, yellows, reds, walks, and waits. The boxes are essential parts of urban infrastructure but are not easily hidden. The Department of Transportation paints them ho-hum gray to try to make them disappear. Why not let artists paint these ubiquitous "canvases," give the neighborhood some identity, and liven the urban landscape a bit?

Fort Collins, Colorado, started such a program in 2004. Other cities have followed suit, including Los Angeles. I encountered several hundreds of examples of this sort of artwork on my trek and marveled at the imagination, skill, and widely varied themes these mini murals demonstrate. Sometimes the "walk" light intended for me came and went before I finished circling and taking pictures. My favorites were ones whose images bent around the box's corner and continued onto the next surface. In the Hermon neighborhood, northeast of downtown, a dragon not only wraps around all four sides but then completes its presence on a second box ten feet away.

Similarly positioned boxes in San Pedro each depict a large eye with a rainbow of tears streaming toward the pavement, message uncertain. Imaginary animals and bright flower blossoms are commonly depicted. Dogs with jetpacks add whimsy. Another box

in Hermon has 60-some brief affirmative statements—covering all sides and the top of the box—describing Hermonites. "We are peaceful. We are collaborative. We are outdoorsy. We are celebratory. We are communal. We are ..." and many more, which in combination make the residents seem like nice people.

Their density varies by area. I found them frequently in the northeast neighborhoods of Highland Park and Hermon and sometimes in Venice, where every flat vertical surface seems to beg for paint. The boxes remain ho-hum gray in many other areas. I wondered if this artistry was authorized, but I figured it had to be in most cases, because these elaborate endeavors would have required multiple days, plenty of time for a highly visible rogue Rembrandt to be arrested. In fact, it is more than authorized, it is regulated.

Should you want to paint a box in LA, identify which box you want to embellish and submit a draft of your artwork to that area's council district office. If the Department of Transportation seconds the approval, then you are ready to go. Well, almost. Your masterpiece cannot "puncture, etch, bend, or otherwise alter the dimensions and integrity of the traffic-signal cabinet." It cannot obstruct air vents, door handles, keyholes, or hinges. It cannot infringe on a trademark or copyright, advertise a business, resemble a stoplight or regulatory sign, cause a glare, make a political statement, portray obscenity, or denigrate public servants or "any living creature protected under the Federal Endangered Species Act." There's more, but that is the idea. We need more sunflowers and dogs with jetpacks.

Paint is easy to apply but tends to fade or peel over time, and if covered over, the artistry is likely gone forever. Contrasted to paint, mosaics are more tedious to create but are more durable. I encountered some exceptional ones on my trek, several almost 2000 years old.

Of course, these oldsters were not made in Los Angeles—they were made in ancient Rome. And I found them on display at the Getty Villa. J. Paul Getty made a fortune in petroleum and spent part of it collecting art, initially displaying it in his home overlooking the Pacific Ocean in the Pacific Palisades neighborhood of LA. He quickly ran out of room and built the Getty Villa down the hill from the original gallery. Its design was inspired by several ancient villas. It is an idyllic combination of buildings, courtyards, water features, and Roman-style gardens all fanned by sea breezes and with the ocean visible in the distance.

The Villa is home to Getty's collection of Greek, Roman, and Etruscan art. His vast, and equally priceless collection of more recent art is exhibited at the Getty Center, which is situated high in the Santa Monica Mountains in the Brentwood neighborhood of LA. Alas, the Center is too far from the city's boundary to be a stop on my trek. Perhaps, however, its exclusion is a benefit, because a visit and description would merit a book of its own.

The same is true for the Getty Villa, and I will not try to describe its collection in any detail. But for anyone who thinks that LA is glitzy, fluffy, and superficial, they need to spend half a day at each Getty venue. Both are breathtaking world-class treasures that combine the best of location, architecture, and collections. Take note, admission is free, but parking is $25. For my adventure, the Getty Villa was my first stop for that day and was easily accessible by bus ($0.75 for seniors). Once I checked my trekking poles and day pack, I looked pretty much like the other visitors.

I'll describe two outstanding mosaics.

With tens of thousands of tiny dark gray and off-white stone squares, the first one depicts monstrous Medusa coiffed with entirely undisciplined curls rather than snakes. Her image is centered in a field of spiraling circles with alternating dark and light triangles that create an illusion of dizzying motion. The other one, in multiple shades of brown and gray, depicts two nude boxers and a white bull that one of the boxers, outfitted with metal-weighted gloves, has just struck dead with a single blow.

As I reclaimed my pack and poles, I reflected on my own boxing lesson and how pedestrian it was by comparison—no weighted gloves, glowering bovine, or birthday suit. I reluctantly left the Villa and walked on.

In Highland Park in the far northeastern area of Los Angeles, a series of four-by-seven-foot mosaics made from irregularly shaped tiles in vivid colors are imbedded in the sidewalks along Figueroa Street. This traditional working-class neighborhood is becoming gentrified, and the 14 mosaics, commissioned by the Department of Transportation, preserve elements of its past, including the Red Car trolleys, a historic women's club, the Highland Theatre, and the beloved Chicken Boy. This 22-foot-tall, muscular, fowl-headed figure in jeans and T-shirt originally promoted a chicken restaurant in another location, but now incongruently stands atop a Mexican restaurant on Figueroa. Sometime before his fiberglass fails, Chicken Boy would make a zany match for Clownerina in Venice.

Venice has a mosaic attraction of its own, which the owners open by appointment for tours on Saturdays. I have chosen to describe it here rather than in Chapter 6 (Venice) where I awarded this wacky beachside neighborhood the bronze medal for attraction density.

Venice didn't need the Mosaic Tile House to reach its award-deserving status, and a description of this unique edifice, along with its front and side yards, sidewalk railing, entry gate, and interior seemed to fit better here. Every surface is tiled with ceramic bits or splinters of colored glass. The artist-owners, she with bright orange hair, started tiling a bathroom in this entirely nondescript bungalow in 1996. He was stymied when standard four-inch squares would not fit properly where a wall met the bathtub, so he broke some pieces to fit. The genie was released. With a whimsical sense of humor, they have embedded ceramic figurines, coffee mugs stacked fifteen high, mirror shards, and heat-flattened wine bottles into every surface except the roof, which would likely collapse from the weight. They say, however, that their masterpiece is still a work in progress, so maybe the roof is fair game. I hope in time that they donate it to an institution so that it can be preserved.

That is what happened to Simon Rodia's labor of love in Watts. He was an Italian immigrant and a tile mason who over 33 years, beginning in 1921, indulged in folk art extraordinaire, ending with 17 conical towers ranging as tall as 99 feet. He made them in his spare time from reinforcing bar wrapped in wire mesh, then covered them with grouted-in tile remnants brought home from work. He also added broken pottery, shells, mirrors, green 7 Up bottles, and colorful rocks that he picked up during long walks and those that neighborhood kids brought by.

In ill health and tired of battling with officials over building permits, Rodia deeded the property to a neighbor and moved away in 1955. The house burned down a year later. The towers survived, but the building department ordered that they be dismantled. Wide outcries of protest led to engineering tests that proved the towers were not in danger of toppling. The City of LA and the State of California finally relented and agreed that this masterpiece in folk sculpture, perhaps the nation's best-known work in this genre, was worth preserving.

Scaffolding was in place when Tammie and I visited, and four highly trained and highly skilled art preservationists from the Los Angeles County Museum of Art were about halfway through a multi-year restoration project. They started by meticulously photographing every surface and cataloging loose and fallen decorations. After the rebar core, which Rodia had merely secured with wire, was welded together, the restorationists were securing all the embellishments in place with a special grout that should last for ages.

When I told friends that I was going to walk to the Watts Towers, I received a lot of advice about why I shouldn't go there, even though they had not ever been anywhere nearby themselves. Yes, Watts was probably an unsafe neighborhood in 1965 when rioting occurred and much of it burned. The reputation for this area south of downtown sustained another blow from the riots that followed the police beating of Rodney King in 1992. But that was over 30 years ago, and Watts has changed into a working-class neighborhood. Some of the single-story bungalows are now being replaced with modern, two-story homes, which bode well for continued neighborhood improvement. I was touched by several homes directly across the street from the Watts Towers. Apparently mosaic-tile mania is contagious, because their low front walls and driveway columns support tiled images that included palm trees and a duck in a puddle. Tammie and I thought Simon would approve.

Walking through Watts we did not notice any homes, old or new, that could be labeled architecturally distinctive. There are other areas around LA's boundary, however, that do have designated noteworthy and strikingly beautiful structures, even though I cannot accurately describe their styles.

I will start in the Tujunga neighborhood, at the foot of Mt. Lukens in the far northeastern corner of LA.

From the beginning, Tujunga attracted independent-minded people who had little patience for building codes and inspectors. Local river rock was abundant, and with a strong back and some bags of mortar mix, one could quickly build a solid home. It was an architectural free-for-all. Or maybe it should be considered an architect-optional zone. For instance, one of the remaining tiny stone homes sits on Fairgrove Avenue. (Most eventually came down in earthquakes.) Directly across the street stands a two-story block-shaped home that has been described as "Spanish Colonial Revival, Art Deco, and Viennese Secessionist." Huh?

Several blocks away, I marveled at a squat house that seems to have been built by a hobbit—stone foundation, bare wood timbers pegged together, ornate lead-glass windows, and a rippling roof topped off with a round chimney made of brick and stone. Even Venice could never top the mix of architectural styles evident in the Tujunga neighborhood.

A noteworthy home in Highland Park, about 15 miles south along LA's eastern border, is called Abbey San Encino. The builder-owner ran a newspaper printing business. Since its completion in 1921, it has always been a private residence rather than a monastery, as its name might imply. The day I walked by, it looked like it was in good shape, but it was locked tight behind a chain-link gate.

The home is made of local river stone, but compared to Tujunga's free-for-all style, this one is well-proportioned. Its terracotta tiled roof, bell tower, and arched entry and loggia all complement each other, making the home look like it might have been nestled in the hills of Tuscany for centuries. A round stained-glass window on the front heightens this impression. It depicts a monk reading a manuscript and a Native American operating a printing press. The window was made less than a mile away at Judson Studios, which is historic in its own right and is listed in the National Register of Historic Places. A visit requires a reservation, so I returned on another day for a tour.

Judson Studios dates to 1897 and is now owned and operated by the great-great-great grandson of the founder. (Judson Studios is the only fifth-generation business I came across on my trek. The family at ABC Caskets now extends into its fourth generation, and third-generation owners manage Tampico Spice and Trim 4 Less.) Judson Stsudios has 500 colors for residential, liturgical, commercial and public clients to choose from for new windows and to replace missing pieces in windows in need of restoration. The steps for making a new window are to settle on a design, print it

full scale, lay the print flat on a large table, cut by hand the glass pieces to match the print, surround all the glass pieces with mini lead I beams, solder the beams together, and waterproof both sides by rubbing grout in the crevices. Restoration involves the same steps after the window has been completely disassembled and each piece of glass scraped clean of old grout.

They don't shirk from large jobs. They had just completed restoring a 22- by 23-foot barrel-vaulted window from the Missouri Capitol Rotunda—a multi-million-dollar project that took two years.

Most of the artisans at Judson Studios have worked there for decades and seem almost trance-like in their devotion to this meticulous work. The ones I talked to all have stained-glass windows at home. Kyle, the project manager and tour guide, pointed out that in an ordinary painting or mosaic, one sees only the light that is reflected off the surface, whereas in a work of stained glass, light coming through the medium produces an entirely different effect.

I left with a heightened appreciation for the craft and wondered if I had overlooked any examples along my trek. I knew that Frank Lloyd Wright often incorporated stained-glass windows into his residential designs, but while he designed several homes in the LA area, none along the city boundaries. Earlier architects of Victorian and craftsman homes also used these embellishments. I decided that stained glass was one more attraction to be on the lookout for.

In the 1960s, ornate Victorian homes in LA were bulldozed with alarming frequency because the existing historic cultural monument program could only register but not protect them. Fortunately, eight great examples were purchased and moved to Heritage Square, an architecture museum located about halfway between downtown LA and Pasadena, just to the right of the Arroyo Seco Parkway. (If you are a passenger in a car headed toward Pasadena, you can glimpse the museum's homes through the trees. If you are driving, it's best to keep your eyes on the serpentine, narrow roadway.)

These architectural gems allow a glimpse of what upscale living in LA was like in the late-19th and early-20th centuries. The interiors of several are furnished and open for tours. All the homes are well-maintained and brightly painted and are aligned as if they originally stood together on a Main Street somewhere.

Across the way, an imported 1875 train depot serves as a gift shop. At the far end, A Methodist church stands next to a recreation of the Colonial Drug Store that originally stood almost directly across the Arroyo Seco Parkway at Avenue 57 and Figueroa. (One of the sidewalk mosaics I mentioned earlier is at that intersection.) The drug store's preserved interior includes a soda fountain with six stools. The original wooden and glass cabinets display 80,000 items that were available to salve or cure any ailment imaginable. Heritage Square is an amiable place to spend a few hours.

Another pleasant place to visit is the home of Charles and Ray Eames, who were a husband-and-wife team of design gurus. This icon of midcentury modern architecture is located in the Pacific Palisades neighborhood of LA, three miles down the coast from the Self-Realization Shrine followed by a short jaunt up a hill.

In 1945, *Arts and Architecture* magazine challenged architects to design modern but modestly priced homes in Southern California for soldiers returning from World War II and their families. The Eames owned a 1.5-acre lot on a bluff facing the ocean and planned to build Case Study House Number Eight there for the competition. The front part of the property was fairly level, and the back portion was steeply sloped. The magazine set up a challenge to build entirely from steel fabricators' wartime and industrial off-the-shelf parts, but such parts turned out to be in short supply. This gave Ray and Charles three years to picnic and play games on their property before construction began, and in the course of doing so they decided on a different plan and location for their house.

With the aid of an eight-foot-tall retaining wall to push the hillside back, they sited the house far back on the property, leaving a row of eucalyptus trees (planted 60 years previously by Abbot Kinney, founder of Venice) and a large, park-like expanse of usable recreation area out front. Two steel and glass boxes, both two stories tall, were arranged side by side, the longer one was the Eames' home and the shorter one their studio. The structures became landmarks of midcentury modern architecture. The couple lived there for the rest of their lives—30 more years for Charles, 40 for Ray.

The property is now managed by the Eames Foundation and is open for tours by reservation several days a week. Visitors are not allowed inside the house, but this matters little, because with the large glass sliding panels open, one can easily see inside and appreciate the Eames's eclectic display of furniture, works of art, and interesting "things" from which they drew inspiration for their industrial designs. These designs revolved principally around chairs, particularly ones made from molded plywood. You have probably sat in one but may not have realized it was designed in a eucalyptus grove in Pacific Palisades. Likewise, any architect designing a modern building in the 1950s and 1960s undoubtedly took inspiration from Case Study House Number Eight.

Other historic homes are dotted about, and some are protected now by neighborhood-initiated Historic Preservation Overlay Zones. I'll mention two when I finally award the gold medal for attraction density. For now, I want to mention several interesting nonresidential structures I encountered.

I was not particularly successful in visiting historic schoolhouses. A one-room one in Santa Monica Canyon is on the grounds of a modern grade school and is fenced off from lookie-loos like me. It presently serves as a library.

I asked two gardeners about the exact location of another one-roomer on the campus of Roscoe Elementary School in Sun Valley. They told me that it had been torn down a month previously.

Finally, I did get to see one. It is on the fully enclosed and extensive campus of El Sereno Middle School, just a couple of miles east of Heritage Square. A custodian walked me from the front office across the campus to this well-kept structure of several rooms situated behind an iron fence and topped with a bell tower and bell. It is listed on the National Register of Historic Places, and the bronze plaque indicates the school is of the Queen Anne revival style and was completed in 1894. Both relics, the school and I, seemed completely invisible to the students walking by. Time flies.

Old theaters also have architectural charms, and three of them were on my route. All are shuttered, fates unknown, at least to me.

One is the Highland Theatre. That is how it is spelled in large capital letters perched on top of a not particularly attractive boxy structure on Figueroa Street in Highland Park. It opened in 1924 and was a proper movie palace and live theater with seating for 1450. There is some interesting geometric detail on its façade, and its style is described as Moorish/Spanish Colonial Revival. The outside is immortalized in one of the aforementioned nearby sidewalk mosaics. The interior featured murals, frescoes, ornate metalwork and moldings, and a vintage balcony. Most of the interior details were apparently covered up during the theater's conversion to a triplex.

Another theater is the Warner Grand, on 6th Street, which was formerly the main shopping street in San Pedro. Warner Brothers Studio built this one and two other Art Deco/Moderne "neighborhood picture palaces." Opening in 1931, the Warner Grand could seat 1500 patrons between the main floor and a mezzanine lounge and balcony. It is still used occasionally for special events. The entry from the sidewalk is made of black and white checkerboard-patterned marble tiles, and the ceiling is an ornate array of repeating raised octagons containing circles with a floral motif. I would love to see the inside. Pictures on the internet imply it was done in truly grand Art Deco exuberance, with stenciled ceilings, etched-glass chandeliers, and tiled fountains.

Finally, there is the Loyola Theater, on Sepulveda Boulevard just north of the Los Angeles International Airport. Plaques for the Flight Path Hall of Fame are right there. Contrasted with the others, its entryway and ticket booth are plain, but the façade is the most elaborate of the three. It features graceful Art Nouveau curves and a 60-foot-tall swan-neck tower rising above the marquee. The building is a designated historical monument. It opened in 1946 and closed in 1982. Then, for a while, it was a church before the interior was gutted and converted into medical office space. The sign out front now says it's for lease. Sigh.

Another interesting commercial building that has not fallen onto such hard times is the Coca Cola Building in South LA. It looks like a ship, complete with portholes, catwalks, a bridge, and hatch-like doorways. The style is called Streamline Moderne, a form of Art Deco, which was popular in the 1930s. It incorporated long horizontal lines and sleek rounded forms to imply modernity. It found its way into the design of the "Coke Building" and from toasters to locomotives.

One such locomotive of the Streamline Moderne form is parked in Sylmar, in the northwest corner of LA and far from Griffith Park and Travel Town, where this sleek engine's aunts and uncles are gathered. This loco's location seemed entirely out of context in this light industrial neighborhood where a nearby warehouse is labeled

American Nuts. The locomotive's owner, JB Nethercutt, was also a nut, in the respectful sense of meaning fanatic.

Nethercutt made a fortune by joining his aunt, Merle Norman, in her cosmetics business. In addition to acquiring one iron horse, he started collecting cars, 120 of which are on display in the Nethercutt Museum, which flanks his locomotive. These beautifully crafted and meticulously restored vehicles clearly demonstrate the transition from boxy-functional forms of the 1920s to the streamlined, closed-cabin cars of the 1930s and beyond.

While a volunteer continued feather dusting a 1933 Duesenberg, he motioned around and said that for 30 years he had painted these cars during their restoration, and he now enjoyed just being around them and keeping them pristine. He noted that Nethercutt's most treasured cars were on display across the street in the Nethercutt Collection, and visiting there required a reservation.

I returned on another day and toured the Collection. Perhaps 20 cars rest on the marble floor of this two-story-high marble-columned palace, designed to resemble a swanky automotive sales room from times gone by. (I felt out of place without a top hat, monocle, and spats.) As before, neither a fleck of rust nor a nick of paint was in sight anywhere, just gleaming surfaces and artful workmanship—entirely world-class. The guide said that the restorations, all performed on site except for the chrome, glass, and tires, required two to three years, and that many of the vehicles had won "best in show" awards at prestigious car shows.

All of the cars are operational and are started at least once a year after their batteries are reinserted and the rust-resistant vinegar in the gas tanks has been replaced with gasoline.

Having completed the tour, I walked out in Great-Gatsby-like awe. Names of long-gone marques like Hupmobile, Peerless, Moon, Franklin, and Bugatti rattled around in my head. I wondered if modern brands such as Tesla, Rivian, and Lucid would be around a hundred years from now.

Another art form I witnessed was far more fleeting, perhaps even more so than my stab at mural painting on the Venice Art Wall. Although transient, this display repeats itself on sunny days. Sidewalk shadows cast by fences produce some amazing patterns, unseen by motorists and available to walkers who are willing to stop and marvel.

CHAPTER 14

PROTECTION

Nidorf Juvenile Hall, where errant youth are temporarily housed pending court dates or placement services, is surrounded by a ten-foot-high brick wall topped with intimidating coils of razor wire. (I did not notice the shadows cast by these metal strips, probably ominous.) Shadows or not, those barriers hint that "Hall" might be euphemistic and that egress, or, in my case, ingress, would not be easy. The guard at the entry kiosk, replete with a bulletproof vest and sidearm, listened to my request, which he eventually elevated up two levels of authority. All answers were polite "no's."

In San Pedro several months later, I tried visiting the Federal Correction Institution, Terminal Island, a low-security facility for 850 male inmates. I guess that the men there are more rambunctious than the teens at Nidorf because the Terminal Island facility is protected by two 12-foot-high chain-link fences spaced 15 feet apart with three-foot-deep coils of razor wire filling space between them. The outer

barrier is topped with another round of barbs. Altogether it seemed like more than minimum security to me, and I later learned that the razor wire was an afterthought and mostly for show to counter the facility's nickname—Club Fed. To score a tour of the correction facility on Terminal Island, I filled out forms online to register as a journalist. I never heard back from them.

On reflection, I rationalized my failure three ways: the interior of one prison probably looks pretty much like another, I had seen plenty on TV, and of all the attractions that this book might entice its readers to visit, prisons were probably low priority.

I was, however, successful at gaining access to a lifeguard station. It was a chilly, overcast afternoon, nobody was on the beach, and the lifeguard seemed happy to have company. I missed where he was maintaining his gaze until he pointed out a single watersport enthusiast far beyond the breaking surf who was zipping through the swells on some sort of board. Even without a sail or kite, it looked as if he was speeding along several feet above the water. In fact, he was.

The lifeguard explained hydrofoil surfing to me. Mounted about two feet underneath a surfboard, a hydrofoil includes an electric motor and propeller. Batteries in the board provide power, and once underway, several quick deep knee bends set the hydrofoil to work, which silently lifts the board out of the water. It is far faster and more maneuverable than a paddle board, and although maybe not as much fun as a jet ski, it would certainly be quieter and more transportable.

Police stations are places that most people, including me, generally like to avoid. But one in Highland Park, a neighborhood in the northeast section of LA, has been converted into a museum, so I figured it might be more interesting than intimidating.

The building is a two-story, symmetrical brick cube with a low-pitched roof. But because it is the only remaining police station in LA from the 1920s, it is often used as a filming backdrop.

I walked out an hour later with mixed feelings. The building, of some architectural interest, served as the precinct station from its completion in 1925 until it was deemed seismically unsafe and abandoned in 1983. Falling on tough times, the structure suffered from fire, water, and vandal damage and was slated for demolition. Historically minded friends obtained a listing for it on the National Register of Historic Places and saved it from destruction. Then, restored by the Los Angeles Police Historical Society, it now recounts LAPD's "road to becoming the most professional police department in the world." That is according to the Historical Society's web page. Having lived in LA for over 40 years and witnessing the serious problems the LAPD has had during that time, I wondered who was offering such accolades.

Nonetheless, the museum bordered the city limits and was worth a look. A couple of school groups were doing the same.

A few steps beyond the front desk were several bare-bone holding cells that fit my mental image of such enclosures and did not include any design features that would make me feel good about being there. Farther on, large glass cases showed how LAPD uniforms and badges have morphed through the ages. Other cases displayed vast arrays of firearms.

Several rooms were devoted to epic events in LAPD history.

The first occurred in 1963. During a traffic stop, two plainclothes officers were overpowered and driven to a rural area where one was murdered and the other ran through the dark to safety. Years later, the event was turned into a book and then a movie by the same name, *The Onion Field.*

The second saga revolved around the Symbionese Liberation Army's kidnapping of Patty Hearst in 1974, the apparent brainwashing she experienced, the crime spree that followed, and the LAPD shootout three months later that left six terrorists dead.

Okay, I get it. Both stories were newsworthy and still resonate with those old enough to remember them. But we are a diminishing number. In stark contrast to the photographs, diagrams, and extensive descriptive text of these events, there was not a peep about Rodney King's brutal beating by LA police officers in 1994. That event and the riots that followed should never be forgotten.

Nonetheless, several exhibits made me smile. One was an enlarged clipping from a 1927 issue of the *LAPD Bulletin* under the heading ARREST THESE PERSONS:

WILLIS MILLER, alias "BOOTS MILLER." . . . Roots of hair light brown, ends having the appearance of being blond or sun-bleached, combed straight back pompadour style; . . . Usually wears blue denim overalls, checked shirt and Western hat with wide brim and three or four dents coming to a peak at the top (size about 7 1/8); loud colored silk handkerchief around neck, heavy black leather boots with fancy green work near the top . . . If in street clothes, may have gray mixed or blue suit of good style with bow tie, black hat and black patent leather "gaiter" shoes with no laces; usually caries revolver and while riding a .30.30 rifle.

If Raymond Chandler did not incorporate this character into one of his novels, he should have. I can imagine Philip Marlowe confronting Boots and saying, "No shoestrings. Hmmm . . . Let me check your hat size."

A sign near the holding cells recalls the days when phone numbers had personalities: "AFTER THE BOOKING PROCESS YOU MAY USE THE PAY TELEPHONE WITHIN LEGAL LIMITATIONS. IF YOU WISH TO OBTAIN THE SERVICES OF A LAWYER OR BAIL AGENT YOU MAY CONTACT A REFERRAL SERVICE AT MADISON 8-1161."

Parked out back was an interesting array of police vehicles including a paddy wagon and cruisers of several vintages, one marred with bullet holes. A heavy-duty truck with a large metal sphere on its bed had mudflaps stating, "BOMB SQUAD STAY BACK 300 FEET." ("No problem, Officer.") A small, rubber-tired tank with a massive prod extending from the front was labeled "LAPD RESCUE VEHICLE." Why this one had been mothballed was not clear. Maybe, because without a place for a social worker to ride, it wasn't an effective problem solver once it busted through a door.

By contrast, when firefighters break down doors, the inhabitants are almost always overwhelmingly happy to see them. The Paul Bunyanesque axes these saviors employ are on display at two LA Fire Department Museums that were on my route. The first, Old Fire Station 36, sits in the middle of the attraction-rich San Pedro. The second one, the African-American Firefighter Museum, p reviously LAFD Station 30, is located in South LA, not far south of downtown and across the street from the historic Coca Cola Building. A third LAFD museum, is too far inside the LA city limits for me to visit on my walk. I did, however, drive there on a non-walking day because I had enjoyed visiting the other two so much.

Like the Police Museum, all three of these fire museums are in square brick buildings dating from the early- to mid-20th century. All of them became obsolete as building codes tightened to better resist earthquakes. Thoughtful city planners recognized that firefighters and police should be at the ready even if other structures were damaged and in need of relief, so they built new fire and police stations. The old fire stations make great museum spaces, complete with brass poles and large garage doors. As firefighting equipment and trucks become dated, it makes perfect sense to display them in decommissioned firehouses staffed by retired firefighters who enjoy the camaraderie, nostalgia, and opportunity to educate visitors in their home away from home.

Here are some interesting things I learned.

When horses pulled fire wagons, the animals were kept in stalls built in the same area that housed the fire engines and were cared for by the firefighters. When the alarm sounded, the horses would automatically leave their stalls and stand at the ready in front of the fire wagons. Their harnesses, suspended from the ceiling, dropped down and could be quickly fastened. Off they went, flanked by the firehouse Dalmatian. This breed was chosen because of its compatibility with horses. Once the engines were in place at the scene of the fire, the horses would be detached and taken a safe distance away, where "Sparky" would keep them calm.

Other dog breeds, often black Labradors, still work for the fire department and go to work after a fire is extinguished. They are trained as arson dogs and can locate and identify accelerants.

Fire grenades were used in the late 19th and early 20th centuries. Essentially reverse Molotov cocktails, they were throwable fragile glass containers that would break on impact and release salt water or other fire suppressants. These were for homes and businesses and were often displayed as colorful and decorative mantel pieces until they were thrown into action before the fire wagons arrived. Fire grenades were eventually replaced by the metal fire extinguishers used today.

Over many centuries, bucket brigades predated any fire hoses, trucks, and grenades. The early human-powered pumps were replaced in the 19th century by ones driven by steam, but their effectiveness was hampered by the amount of time it took for water to boil. Therefore, while the horse-drawn fire truck was at the station, hot water from the building was continuously circulated through the engine's boiler. When the alarm sounded, the connection separated automatically, and a hot fire was started in the truck's firebox with the idea that steam pressure sufficient to power the pump would be available by the time the team reached the fire. The plaque describing this "steamer" concludes with this statement. "Road speed: dependent on ruts in the road, the grades encountered, and the temperament of both horses and driver." Diesel motors put an end to those concerns.

Secured to the side of one of the fire engines and folded in half for compactness was a life net, a trampoline whose supports were provided by a ring of firefighters. It was invented in 1887 and is credited with saving the lives of people jumping from as high as six stories and occasionally higher. It was, however, fraught with dangers. One of the less gruesome stories is about hotel guests throwing their suitcases out first and then injuring themselves by landing on their hard luggage. The advent of hook and ladder trucks reduced the need for life nets, and the appearance of inflatable jumping cushions made life nets completely obsolete. The pillow has saved the lives of people jumping from as high as ten stories.

In an earlier time, soiled "turnout gear"—a firefighter's protective pants and jacket—was viewed positively as a sign of participation, and all the garb was kept upstairs by the beds. It was eventually discovered, however, that the gear harbored carcinogens, so now all the turnout gear is cleaned regularly and kept downstairs with the fire engines.

Today's firefighting equipment includes helicopters and fire boats. It makes sense, but I was surprised to learn that LAFD helicopter pilots and divers are firefighters first and then develop their more specialized skills. Separate skills are required for the firefighter who roosts on the tail end of a hook and ladder truck. The tillerman, err... tiller person, takes pains to keep the behemoth from cutting corners and clipping power poles and traffic lights.

This brings me to the history of women and Black people of both sexes in the LAFD, a history that is preserved in many old photographs and descriptions at the museums.

Several companies of volunteer women were established in 1912 with the awareness that many men worked downtown or in the industrial areas during the day, leaving a shortage of men to fight fires in outlying areas. It was not until 1983, however, that a female recruit, Cynthia Barbee, successfully completed the requirements and became the first paid female firefighter. A year later, d'Lisa Davies, became the first Black female firefighter to serve in the LAFD. Black men started much earlier but met with great resistance. Sam Haskins was born a slave in Virginia and came to California in 1880 and joined the LAFD in 1892, the first Black man to do so, but it was only a part-time job. He was killed en route to a fire three years later when he lost his balance and was thrown into the large wheel alongside the boiler on a steam engine.

Two years later, George Bright was the first Black full-time firefighter. He rose through the ranks and was promoted to Lieutenant in 1902. To avoid having Bright command white firefighters, the department gathered up all the Black and Mexican firemen and formed the first non-white fire company. At a time of changing demographics in LA, this unit was transferred from an all-white area to an emerging mixed-race neighborhood. It became Engine Company 30, located in the building that is now the African-American Firefighter Museum. Abject segregation remained until 1955, but even for years after, Black firefighters were met with extreme hostility in the mixed-race firehouses, including being forced to eat separately and provide their own kitchen utensils and supplies. Little did I know that visiting fire museums would be a lesson in the history of racism in Los Angeles.

Another surprise awaited me as I walked onto the campus of Cal State University at Los Angeles. It is five miles east of downtown and perched atop a bluff with cars racing along on the Long Beach and San Bernadino Freeways below. Set off by itself, the first building I encountered was a four-story modern building—the Hertzberg-Davis Forensic Science Center. I walked in and learned from the display cases in the front hall that this was "the largest municipal regional collaborative crime lab facility in the nation." A display of historic photographs included ones of Frank Sinatra being fingerprinted, mug shots of Fatty Arbuckle, and a vintage mug shot of other suspects whose face and profile images were captured together on one piece of (expensive) film through the use of a mirror placed at an angle behind their heads. A case that serves as a gift shop (shouldn't every crime lab have a gift shop?) displayed a T-shirt that said, "Keep calm and swab on."

The Forensic Science Center serves the LA Police Department and LA County's Sheriff's Department. Located on Cal State LA's campus, it has a close working relationship with the university's faculty and students in the criminology and criminal justice program, which offers both bachelors and masters degrees, internships, and research opportunities. Students can also obtain certificates in crime scene investigation and friction ridge (fingerprint) examination. Access to the building beyond the front hall was controlled by security guards, and, not feeling that leaving traces of my DNA would in any way benefit me, I walked on, careful not to touch the glass door with my fingers.

As off limits to city line walkers as the crime lab seemed to be, by contrast, the SQRD Lab was entirely welcoming. Google Maps identified its location in the Harbor Gateway North neighborhood, close to where the "Shoestring" attaches to LA proper but did not reveal its purpose. From the street, the windowless black brick building with brightly painted triangles was equally unrevealing.

Tammie and Michael were walking with me that day. We went around back and were buzzed in from the parking lot by the lab director. I explained my trek and introduced my friends. He reacted almost as if he had been expecting us and gave us a 30-minute tour of the lab. Marijuana is legal in California, and SQRD tests its potency and purity. He explained that legitimate cannabis growers must have their weed inspected and certified. SQRD, whose name is some play on "squared" that I did not understand, tests not only the leaves, but also their products—which include beverages, lotions, chocolates, and gummies.

The lab techs will take small quantities from every 50 pounds of the product to be evaluated, pulverize it, test its potency, and look for contaminants. High on the walls in this building's open interior were labels identifying the testing equipment that look for nasties such as pesticides, residual solvents, molds, and heavy metals.

Steamer-trunk-sized automated testing machines sat on counters with larger ones on the floor. They were humming along and likely sending and receiving messages from an array of attached computers. Liquid-carrying tubes and large ventilation ducts added to the impressive complexity.

In a separate room labeled Microbiology, refrigerator-sized incubators housed culture samples that might grow mold or bacteria, such as *E. coli* and *salmonella*. The lab director speculated that only 20% to 30% of marijuana sold in California has been assessed and certified. Knowing what I learned at SQRD, I fear for the health of those who are using illegal products.

Compared to police and fire emergency services, which are highly visible and audible, marijuana labs do not similarly enter our conscience. There are other services of order and protection—monumental, critical, ubiquitous—that also normally fly below our radar. These foils to urban disorder are its infrastructure—the glue that holds a city together and keeps it running.

CHAPTER 15

INFRASTRUCTURE

Function here takes precedence over form. Often not aesthetically pleasing, infrastructure typically gets shoved to the city's edges or sunk beneath its streets.

Water is a prime example. We turn on the tap, fill a glass, take a drink, and send the remainder down the drain without giving much, if any, thought regarding its origin or fate. Earlier I described the California Aqueduct and its delivery of water from afar that has allowed Los Angeles to flourish. Let's look at some other underappreciated elements of infrastructure that I encountered along LA's borders.

Our tidy prehistoric ancestors tossed their discarded dinner bones, shells, and pottery fragments into pits. When silted over and sealed from erosion, these middens became treasure troves for archeologists trying to understand the lives of early humans. With the advance of civilization and the rise of towns and cities, our more recent ancestors pitched their refuse into the streets, which solved the immediate problem but meant that nothing was left for archeologists. When the gutter became an unacceptable solution (or maybe it was because sewers were no longer open), people turned to burning their trash, which vexes archaeologists.

Even though the smoke was noxious, backyard incineration continued into the 1950s in Los Angeles, when automobile exhaust began compounding the problems produced by fumes from smoldering garbage. To address the growing scourge of smog and knowing that they could not quell Angelenos' urge to drive, city leaders sought an alternative to burning trash and turned to landfills, a concept that had taken root fifty years earlier.

Americans now depend heavily on landfills, with each person currently contributing on average four to five pounds of rubbish a day. Yes, some refuse is composted, recycled, or burned to generate electricity, but about half is buried in landfills. Will future archeologists be interested in delving through them for artifacts of our current culture? Wanting to find out, I located a landfill inside the Los Angeles city limits.

Sunshine Canyon Landfill hovers just inside LA's northern border. Two freeways intersect nearby, which facilitates access, but the last mile up to the entrance is a two-lane road with narrow shoulders, no sidewalks, and a steady stream of big trucks going in each direction— not pedestrian friendly, but I walked in. The sign at the entrance said nothing about welcoming or not welcoming visitors, so I proceeded.

Once on the property, which according to the map is 1.6 square miles, the road turned uphill, steep enough that the laden trucks were growling as they slowly ascended while the empty ones barreled down. I walked on the going-in side. The canyon wall on my left sloped up moderately, and, at regular intervals, wide horizontally oriented terraces traversed the expanse, giving it the same contour as a step pyramid. On one terrace, a bulldozer was going back and forth, apparently crushing and compacting the refuse (sorry, archeologists) under a layer of soil (sorry, birds and varmints). In the far distance, to the right, and just below the ridge line, I could see a long line of trucks inching along and assumed that was the site of today's delivery action.

About a half mile in, a worker was shoveling mud from a drainage ditch paralleling the drive, and I asked him where "headquarters" was. He gestured up and to the right, and I could see a side road there. When I got to the turn, several signs indicated both Office ahead and No entry without prior authorization. Did that include curious trekkers with day packs and walking sticks? I decided it probably did, so I reluctantly turned around.

I had not gone far before the most mud and dust laden pickup truck imaginable pulled alongside me. No telling what color its paint was. "Hi, nice truck. I'm Roy. I'm walking the LA city limits, and I'm interested in seeing the landfill." "It's too dangerous. We can't allow pedestrians. Let me offer you a ride down." "Okay."

When I got home that evening, I studied the Sunshine Canyon Landfill's website in detail. I learned, for instance, that they weigh each vehicle on entry and exit and charge $98 per ton of household refuse and for construction and demolition waste, more for asphalt and contaminated soil. They monitor each load for radiation and also check to ensure the absence of electronic equipment. "Customers" must have a hard hat and a safety vest, which are each available for purchase on site for $8.27 for the ill-prepared. It dawned on me that I could drive around my neighborhood and pack a couple of old chairs and some broken-up chunks of concrete into my SUV. For a $98 admission ticket and $16.54 for personal protective equipment, I could return triumphantly for a firsthand landfill experience.

On reflection, however, I decided against it. Even though the ruse would let me learn more about landfills, it would not be in keeping with my quest to *walk* the line. So until I can fly a drone over, the day-to-day workings of the Sunshine Canyon Landfill will remain shrouded in mystery, at least for me. I also rationalized my exclusion by reflecting that other points of interest farther along on my trek—the runways at Los Angeles International Airport, for instance—were going to be off limits.

Although active landfills a re n ot a ccessible t o l ookie-loos, i n Chapter 5 (Nurture I described my firsthand look at a former one in Griffith Park—now called the Toyon Canyon Landfill Restoration Project. There, the proponents originally sold the concept of waste management by gushing that the 40-acre leveled-out canyon would be converted to a recreation area for ball sports and picnicking within five years after 9 million cubic feet of rubbish had been sealed off and some areas replanted with California holly (scientific name: Toyon. Protests aside, the landfill opened in 1958 and was finally closed in 1985.

Once decommissioned, garbage-produced methane initially powered five electric generators. By now, the production has dwindled to insignificant amounts, which is burned off. The grid of gas pipes and pumps could be removed in coming decades. A 1968 master plan proposed a nine-hole golf course punctuated by waterways. Ten years later "Toyon Meadow" was going to be a festival site, a trailhead, and perhaps the site for a youth hostel. Don't hold your breath. The experts now say that the land will continue to settle irregularly for decades and not be suitable for any of the dreamed recreations. Imagine, for instance, how a golfer would have trouble reading a green in the middle of a sudden jiggle or if a pitcher had to hurl from a pit rather than a mound. So the area is left to hikers, birders, and equestrians.

Reforestation is not possible because the refuse is capped with a five-foot-thick barrier of densely packed clay. This protects the fill from rainwater seeping in and producing contaminated runoff. Trees with barrier-penetrating roots would require removal. Toyon and native grasses will have a better chance. I'm skeptical that the authorities will have the stomach to remove the collecting pipes and electric generators, which will likely remain as dystopian relics, reminders of the 40 stories of garbage that filled a wilderness canyon—further motivation, I hope, for us to reduce, reuse, recycle.

Los Angeles Sanitation promotes recycling in several forms. It supplies each residence with large green trash barrels, which are emptied weekly. In a city the size of LA, garden trimmings and kitchen waste are composted on an industrial scale at multiple sites. Once tested to ensure the absence of pesticides, disease-causing bacteria, and toxic metals, LASAN makes the resultant TOPGRO soil amendment and mulch products available to residents for free.

The composting facility I visited is in Griffith Park, just over a ridge from the Toyon Canyon landfill. Here LASAN combines green trimmings and chipped wood collected by the park's gardeners with "zoo doo" produced by the zoo's elephants, zebras, camels, and other leaf processors. The resultant compost goes back onto the park's landscape.

When grinding orange peels, chicken bones, and eggshells in the garbage disposal or flushing human waste and medications down the toilet, we may fleetingly, at most, consider the fate of such castoffs. However, when several million people live within smelling and disease-spreading distance of each other, it is paramount that officials take waste management seriously. In regions where clean water is plentiful, handling wastewater may mean just treating it and sending it into a river or ocean. By contrast, in Southern California, where fresh water is scarce and is likely to become more so, waste management is quickly coming to mean reclamation.

My curiosity and thirst, at least for information, led me to the LA Department of Sanitation's Terminal Island Water Reclamation Plant in San Pedro. Andrew Howard, wastewater treatment operator and field trainer, met me, loaned me a hard hat, and took me on a top-to-bottom tour. He told me that because of Southern California's population and its sprawling distribution, LASAN operates the largest wastewater collection system in the US This includes 6,700 miles of sewers (the distance from LA to Beijing) and 140,000 manholes, er, excuse me, maintenance holes. The system services more than 4 million people in a 600-square mile area that includes Los Angeles and 29 contracting cities and agencies.

The plant is one of four operated by LASAN. Combined, they process 580 million gallons of wastewater every day, which would be enough to fill a mile-square pool almost three feet deep. The Terminal Island plant is well-situated. It has only to send its reclaimed water short distances for it to serve useful purposes. The nearby petroleum refineries use large volumes of water for cooling. Also, beginning in the 1940s, drinking water wells in this coastal area had to be abandoned because contaminating seawater was pushing inland. To form a barrier, highly purified reclaimed water is injected underground. This saves 2.2 billion gallons of freshwater annually (a mile-square pool eleven feet deep). More uses for reclaimed water are on the way.

Highly purified reclaimed wastewater results from an intricate series of physical, biological, and chemical processes. The first step is physical. A screen with half-inch gaps between its parallel metal bars removes plastic bags, toys, clothing, sanitary products, sticks, leaves, and similar items that have no business there at all. The grit chamber comes next, where the flow slows to let sand and gravel settle out. Then the water rests in large pools for several hours while surface scrapers slowly skim off oil and grease and bottom scrapers do the same for solids that have drifted down.

The second step is biological. Mixed with microorganisms, the water rests in large, open tanks for up to a day while air bubbles through. This provides a suitable environment for bacteria to complete rapid consumption of dissolved wastes. At the end of their digestion, the wee beasties die, clump together, and settle out.

The third step includes another mechanical cleansing as the water first gravitates slowly through beds of sand and then mixes with sodium hypochlorite (household bleach). Here, traditional wastewater treatment ends, and the clear water drains into a nearby river or ocean. But it likely remains contaminated with pharmaceuticals and other chemicals, viruses, and assorted vile components that make it unsuitable for reuse. Advanced treatment comes to the rescue.

The Terminal Island Water Reclamation Plant is one of the first in the country to use the following additional steps to produce highly purified water. Microfiltration sends the water through tubules made of the same plastic that is often used in yogurt cups, except that these tubules have minute pores, small enough to block the passage of microorganisms. Operators then force the water through membranes with even smaller pores in a process called reverse osmosis. (This was first used in World War II submarines to produce fresh water.) It captures molecules even just slightly larger than H2O molecules that the bleach hasn't destroyed.

Finally, any remaining viruses meet their demise courtesy of exposure to intense ultraviolet light. At this point, lavender-colored pipes, celebrating the water's purity, carry the reclaimed water to its destinations. Today those destinations are the underground saltwater barriers, other aquifers that are sources of drinking water, and refineries and other local industries.

The tour convinced me. At the end, Andrew showed me two taps. One was connected with "city water." The other extended from a lavender pipe. The water from each tasted the same—good, refreshing, no yuck factor. What happens to the extracted biosolids? Some are heated in three-story-tall egg-shaped digesters on site. The process, a form of composting, kills pathogens and produces flammable "biogas," which heats the next batch of biosolids. This digestion produces 50 tons a day of nutrient-rich leftovers, which are

transported to a 4500-acre farm owned by LASAN near Bakersfield, 130 miles away. There it enriches the soil, and the produced grain becomes feedstock for local dairies.

A second portion of the biosolids is pumped a mile deep into the ground near the water treatment plant. There it undergoes a high-temperature, low-oxygen degradation into carbon dioxide, methane, and inert residual solids. The formation's brine captures and retains the carbon dioxide. The methane is a source of renewable energy.

And finally, a third portion of the biosolids goes to LASAN's composting facility in Griffith Park and becomes an ingredient in TOPGRO. Should you want to compete with LASAN on a commercial basis, here is the recipe for making a 15-ton batch of TOPGRO, which LASAN does daily: 4 tons of zoo doo, 20 tons of biosolids, and 50 cubic yards of grass, leaves, and chipped wood. Mix well with an end loader and bulldozer. Stir occasionally for 60 days. Serves untold flowers and shrubs.

Waste management is only one of many infrastructural elements that support civil living. Others involve delivering water, gas, and electricity and providing communication and transportation networks. In other words, these are essential services that enable, maintain, and enhance communal life—the glue that holds a city together and keeps it running. As critical as these elements are, they may be displeasing to one or more of our senses, so they are likely to be buried or at least pushed away from a city's center. That is certainly the case with LA's landfills and water treatment plants, which made them within easy reach as I walked the line. And they take up enough space that they are hard to overlook.

Other essential services may present themselves subtly but are nonetheless important. Here are some that I encountered.

I ran into delivery folk all the time, right there on the sidewalk—employees of UPS, USPS, FedEx, Amazon Prime. "Hi, how many deliveries are you making today?" The Prime drivers were specific. "186." "204." "262." I responded to the one offering the largest number with, "Wow, that must be a record." "No." "Well, then, what has been your biggest day?" "I try not to hold on to that."

The USPS letter carriers cite the most variation, which depends on whether their route is mainly individual residences, apartments, or office buildings. "About 200." "800." "1600." "I have no idea." Some of them, park their truck, walk up one side of a block and down the other, which is good for 15,000 – 20,000 steps a day and about average for me too. A Department of Water and Power meter reader told me one of his routes was 14.5 miles, up and down hills.

I came across an Edison Electric duo flying a drone. I was particularly happy to talk to them because I had just been kicked out of the landfill and was still chagrined. These guys were remotely inspecting and photographing high-voltage electric towers. I didn't ask them what peril their hard hats were protecting them from.

On another day, I found two orange-suited DWP workers in the middle of a weedy vacant lot on a corner not far from LAX. They were using shovels rather than any heavy equipment, and although several signs on the surrounding chain-link fence said Keep Out, it looked safe. My curiosity led me in. They seemed happy to take a break from scraping weeds away on several 10-foot patches, which they said they were doing in preparation for soil sampling.

I learned that the site was slated for an electric-vehicle charging station and current ordinances stipulated that all new developments provide on-site rainwater retention, both to reduce sudden runoff and to enhance groundwater infiltration. The workers were not sure that the charging station was going to come about for two reasons. First, they explained, any cistern to retain water could not come closer than 10 feet to the level of groundwater, which was 34 feet down. Creative engineering could likely surmount that obstacle. But secondly and likely more problematic, they pointed to a large puddle/small pond in the middle of the property. They said that it dries up between rains, but that at least once somebody had observed waterfowl paddling around. In the eyes of the authorities, this makes the puddle/pond a lake. I can only imagine the red tape that could tie up such a project. Do the neighbors want a charging station there? Did somebody really see a duck?

I saw commercial vehicles with CNG stickers on their back bumper everywhere. Compressed natural gas burns much cleaner than gasoline and diesel fuel and seems to have a future in the trend away from petroleum-based fuels. But in 342 miles and walking past numerous conventional filling stations, I came across only one CNG pump, and it was behind locked gates at a storage facility for Commuter Express buses. I am not certain that CNG is ready for Los Angeles automobilistas.

The same seems true for hydrogen, another eco-friendly fuel. I found two pumps. One looked lonely at the far edge of a conventional filling station in Woodland Hills. I wondered who used it and how often they tanked up, so I asked the mopey attendant inside. "It's out there."

I happened upon another hydrogen filling station on the Cal State LA campus, east of downtown, just a stone's throw uphill from the San Bernadino Freeway, also known as the I-10. The station consists of a single pump shaded by a futuristic canopy and next to a low building on the far side of the drive through. Nobody was around. I wanted to learn more, but I had no choice but to walk on. Later I was able to contact Blake Cortis, the station technician, who gave Phil and me a tour on another day. Blake told me that he had been involved in the planning, construction, and operation of the station from the time it was conceived in 2012.

It was a seat-of-the-pants venture to design and build the whole station, beginning with the on-site electrolyzer. It uses electricity generated from natural gas to break down water into hydrogen and oxygen. The hydrogen gas is highly compressed and stored. The oxygen is released into the air. Once in a vehicle, a fuel cell converts hydrogen and atmospheric oxygen into electricity and water. The electricity powers a motor. The car moves. It seems like a roundabout way to motivate an electric vehicle, but in 2012 battery-electric-vehicle technology was in its infancy, and there was a push in California to promote the hydrogen fuel-cell technology. One attraction was that a fill-up took less than ten minutes compared to many hours to fully recharge a battery EV. Hyundai and Honda, among several other manufacturers, did and do sell fuel-cell-electric vehicles, but only in California. On any given day, there are perhaps only 30 to 50 hydrogen filling stations across the entire state that are operational and have a supply of hydrogen available, so not surprisingly BEVs outsell FCEVs by 100 to one.

Even with this bleak reality, Blake did not seem concerned about job security. At the CSLA facility, the emphasis is on research and education rather than consumer service, and the engineering students gain unique firsthand experience that lands them jobs immediately upon graduation with either a bachelor's or master's degree. The fuel-cell technology may find its calling, not in powering personal automobiles, but in larger craft both on land and sea, where the efficiencies and resources are different. As I pulled away in my gas-guzzling SUV, I wondered whether the large letters over the canopy, Hydrogen Station, were informing the past or the future.

Did you notice that in the previous paragraph I wrote *the* San Bernadino Freeway and *the* I-10? Anyone who says, "Harbor Freeway," "5 Freeway," or "Interstate 5," instantly gives it away that they are new to the area. We long-term Angelenos call our divided highways *freeways* and use the article *the* for all of them, as in, "Take *the* 405 and then head west on *the* 118." This regional quirk stems from when the freeway system was in its infancy and these new limited-access highways were paralleling and crisscrossing older routes. So, for instance, a new freeway to Pasadena was supplanting routes 6, 66, and 99, and it was easier to remember and use a descriptive name noting the destination rather than a jumble of numbers. Therefore "Take route 6, or maybe it's called 66 along there, no, it's US 99" became "Take the freeway to Pasadena." For brevity and clarity, the directions morphed. "Take the Pasadena Freeway." Later, the route numbers were consolidated, but the use of the article stuck. There are examples of this convention elsewhere. For instance, what would New Yorkers think if I asked, "How do I get to Bronx?"

Not only do we derive driving guidance from verbal directions for the freeways, signage on surface streets also helps, in more ways than what is evident at first glance. In addition to indicating the streets' names, they let me know if I had wandered across LA's border into Santa Monica, Torrance, Burbank, Pasadena, or any other of the 30-plus cities and unincorporated areas that share boundaries with the City of Angels. That is because all of LA's street signs now consistently have white block letters on a blue background. Glendale uses black lettering on white signs. Burbank uses white lettering on a green background. Santa Monica's signs are white on blue with a yellow stripe across the bottom.

Across the metropolis though, the font is almost universally Highway Gothic, which is designed to be quickly readable, even at a distance. The letters have no "feet," and the tops of the stems of the lower-case b's, d's, k's, l's, and t's are trimmed at an angle. (Walkers have time to take note of these nuances. Drivers, please don't try.)

Upon even closer scrutiny, the vintages of LA street signs reveal themselves. Early on, the street signs were wooden. Those are long gone. In neighborhoods developed in the 1930s through 1950s, the metal signs are rectangular and have two faces with an inch gap between them—a perfect urban roost for small birds. The lettering is all caps with a period at the end of the abbreviation. What followed in roughly 10-year intervals were, first, signs with a mix of upper- and lower-case letters (apparently the first in the country) and abbreviations without periods. Then the black/deep blue background color changed to the present medium blue. More recently, new signs have their inner and outer edges trimmed back at the bottom, which changes the rectangles to trapezoids and makes each sign seem as if it is pointing the way.

Should you be searching for additional cocktail-party topics, segue into this. The font for freeway signs has traditionally been white Highway Gothic lettering on green backgrounds. These are now being changed to a font called Clearview. This is because the glare of headlights and the lettering's reflective paint make it hard, especially for older drivers, to distinguish a's, e's, and o's in Highway Gothic. Clearview makes the openings in the a's and e's larger. When signs in each font are side by side, it is easy to see the difference. What is easier to spot is that Clearview does not trim off the tops of b's, d's, k's, l's, and t's. True, I did not walk along any freeways on my trek, but I walked under and over a number of them and observed the signage from a distance.

However signed, our vast sprawl of roadways caters to drivers' passions for getting into, around, and out of LA as efficiently as possible. Paralleling and crossing under these roadways is another extensive concrete network, but only just for one-way rapid transit out of town and into the ocean. Here is a paradox. On one hand Southern California is naturally arid and sorely dependent on imported water, which has to be rationed in some years. On the other hand, winter rains can suddenly produce an extreme overabundance, which in the past has caused devastating floods as racing water followed changing paths of least resistance across the flatter portions of LA closest to the ocean. Over the past 100-plus years, LA City and County along with the US Army Corps of Engineers have combined forces to retard these episodic gushes of raging water behind large dams and catchment basins and then direct the overflow into concrete-lined channels that hasten its entry into the Pacific Ocean.

These waterways are all below street level and therefore mostly invisible from cars crossing or paralleling their routes. On foot, however, the ubiquity of this network is evident, but their capability is not, since most of the time they are dry or only conveying a trickle. Since I did not walk on rainy days, I only captured an indirect indication of their capacity and the magnitude of the rushing water, demonstrated by plastic bags and other refuse snagged high on the walls of these channels.

At times these waterways are entirely covered over and are accessible to utility workers via maintenance holes. I walked by many of these and began to appreciate their covers as works of urban industrial art—giant cast iron coins. The details of those located in sidewalks are easily appreciated. The ones in the streets often have imbedded asphalt obscuring their patterns and lettering, which is okay, because I know better than to stand in intersections and take pictures of the pavement.

Some of the covers indicate ownership, e.g., LA Water, Metropolitan Water District, LA County Flood Control District, Bell System, So Calif Gas Co. Others announce contents, e.g., Sewer, Electric Power, Storm Drain. I had to ask a utility worker about a couple of cryptic labels. "D" means storm drain, "S" denotes sewage. Some lids proudly record country of origin, e.g., USA, India, Mexico. The patterns vary too. I found big circles containing hexagons, little circles, or squares; concentric circles and starbursts; and several different waffle formats.

You may think I am nuts to find manhole covers interesting, but I am not alone. There are at least two books on the subject. I don't find the topic any more unusual than coin collecting, and manhole-cover fancy is an outdoor, ambulatory activity. What could be better?

Not all infrastructure is designed for humans alone. Across the northern borders of Los Angeles are neighborhoods that are zoned RA—residential agriculture. That means that many of the semirural lots in neighborhoods such as Chatsworth, Sylmar, Sunland, and Tujunga are oversized and can accommodate horses. Not much may be apparent from looking at the fronts of individual homes, but telltale signs are present.

The first one I encountered was a busy intersection with the crosswalk button raised six feet off the ground. It wasn't a mistake, made clear by little sign with a double-ended, horizontal arrow and a silhouetted horse and rider. The button's location obviates the need for an equestrian to lean down and risk falling off to activate the WALK light. Pedestrians will have to reach up. Height-challenged individuals might have to jump, wait for a horse and rider to come by, or take a chance and dash across.

Sandy horse paths crisscross the area and often parallel the streets with sidewalks separating them from vehicular traffic. The paths are further defined by horizontal steel-pipe railings supported on vertical posts that curve in at the top. The railings would bump a horse at chest level and its rider about mid-thigh. I gather that the rails keep the horse from smearing its rider against an unyielding post or wall.

The approaches to some major intersections have Horse Crossing painted in white block letters on the pavement. Then if riders safely make their way to the corner shopping center and want to stop for a latte, a tie rail is conveniently located adjacent to the parking lot for cars.

In the middle of it all, I found a saddle and tack shop—a saddlery, proof that one's expenses following the purchase of a ranchette and horse are far from over. Saddle, bridle, bit and bit cleaner, crop, helmet, boots, spurs, breeches—a daunting display presented to this pedestrian adventurer. I decided to start with a 32-ounce bottle of Mane 'n Tail Shampoo "for shiny and manageable hair" because the clerk, an equestrienne, said it was good for humans too. It's working great so far. I wanted to be looking fine for my visits to the gold-metal Hot Spot.

CHAPTER 16

SAN PEDRO AND WILMINGTON

Nostalgia reigns here. A patch of corn and neat rows of cabbage sit alongside a farmhouse. Out back, laundry is drying on a clothesline. Two blocks way, an industrial area includes a fully equipped machine shop and a railroad roundhouse. Downtown a shingle-roofed railroad station has tracks running along one side. On the other, pickup trucks, sedans, and a Greyhound bus fill the parking lot.

No, this is not San Pedro (remember, PEE-droh) itself but part of the layout of one of its two model railroad clubs. They are located within several Pullman-car lengths of each other in old Army barracks at the decommissioned Fort MacArthur. Both clubs are open for trips down memory lane on Saturdays and are well worth a visit, even for those who have never ridden a train or seen a steam locomotive chugging along.

The Angeles Gate Hi-Railers Model Railroading Club includes the vignettes I mentioned above. Everything is scaled down to where one quarter of an inch on the layout equals a foot in real life. (This is O gauge, famously used by Lionel). At this scale, a person six feet tall is reduced to an inch and a half. The shapes of the vehicles in front of the railway station indicate the era—around 1950. Among thousands of other details, scrutiny reveals a graveyard with markers memorializing deceased club members. These elements are all stationary. What brings the mountain, urban, and industrial scenes to life are the mesmerizing movements and sounds of multiple locomotives pulling long rows of cars through the elaborate panorama—gray and yellow boxcars carrying freight, and sleek silver streamliners transporting tiny plastic passengers. The layout is huge—it takes a train, moving at a simulated 30 miles per hour, 10 minutes to make a complete circuit.

Marveling at the nearby Belmont Shore Model Railroad Club's layout requires even more scrutiny because everything is N scale, meaning that a real-life six-footer stands less than a half inch tall. Compared to my growing-up American Flyer set (S gauge) with its Reading Lines iron horse pulling three cars, the trains at both clubs were much longer and thereby more realistic. One steam engine was pulling 35 cars, and a diesel loco was pulling 12 passenger cars and a diner. The layouts for both clubs are far more extensive than anybody could have at home, and members share the costs of development and maintenance. Members can bring their own locomotives and rolling stock and play engineer.

One enthusiast was replacing his 40 box cars into their carrying case. I asked him what it took to pull all of them, and he pointed to his prized iron horse, about the size of my index finger. It cost $1800 complete with authentic sounds and the ability to simulate steam. It is doubtful that anyone under 60 has seen real coal-burning, smoke-spewing behemoths underway for more than just demonstration. Nonetheless, they have a firm grasp on people's imaginations and are an important part of America's history of westward expansion and economic power. I recommend visiting both clubs for a moving history lesson.

The model railroad clubs set the tone for San Pedro and Wilmington in general—unpretentious, functional, respectful of the past. By contrast, Venice, the winner of my bronze-medal Hot Spot award, is funky, quirky, lively. Griffith Park, the silver medal winner, is horizontally and vertically vast and entirely committed to recreational activities. How then can blue-collar San Pedro and adjacent Wilmington possibly merit the gold-medal Hot Spot award for visitor interest? Look back at the previous chapters' topical categories—relics, water, nature, nurture, flight, reflection, fun, work, art, protection, and infrastructure. San Pedro and Wilmington have unique, and often multiple, examples of each.

We can start by looking at the map of LA's city limits. The whereabouts of San Pedro and Wilmington are instantly identifiable, dangling by the "shoestring" from the nightmare of zigzags that defines the remainder of the city's boundaries. I would defy anybody to point to the exact locations of Tujunga, Sylmar, Playa del Rey, Boyle Heights, and Eagle Rock—all neighborhoods through which I walked and whose attractions I have described. Conversely, even children with no map reading skills could identify San Pedro and Wilmington as easily as pointing to their own noses.

Remember too that this area stood out even before there were maps. The Tongva Indians lived here for millennia. In 1542 the smoke from their cooking fires attracted Juan Cabrillo's attention as he sailed up the coast "discovering" Alta California. Spanish settlement and trade followed. Richard Henry Dana in *Two Years Before the Mast* described the first known commercial structure in San Pedro. Built in 1823, this adobe building warehoused cow hides en route from area missions to Boston. Hence began the Port of LA.

Phineas Banning, a young man from Wilmington, Delaware, was instrumental in the development of what has become the largest container port in the US. He arrived in San Pedro in 1851 at age 21 and started work as a store clerk. He changed to driving stagecoaches between San Pedro and the pueblo of Los Angeles, 20 miles north, which at the time had a population of 2000. Banning recognized opportunity and started his own overland transit company, which eventually grew to transport goods and people between San Pedro and LA, the gold fields near Bakersfield, and 300 miles inland to Yuma in Arizona Territory.

One success led to another. He began expanding the docks and harbor in San Pedro, purchased a square mile of adjacent land for port expansion, and named it Wilmington after his hometown in Delaware. A government-funded breakwater to protect the harbor and dredging to deepen it allowed larger vessels direct access to the docks. Goods no longer had to be ferried across the shallows on smaller craft.

At the beginning of the Civil War, Banning donated a tract of land in Wilmington for the Union Army's Southwest Command headquarters, which became Camp Drum (tents) and later Drum Barracks (wooden buildings). Out of gratitude, Banning received an appointment as a brigadier general and used the title of general for the rest of his life. (Compare that to grandiose self-appointed monikers of the time—The Colonel (Griffith J. Griffith) and The Builder (Hubert Eaton).

Troops were stationed at Drum Barracks to deter the substantial number of Confederacy sympathizers in California. (Locally, southerner John Breckenridge received twice the votes Lincoln did in the 1860 presidential election.) The troops were also placed to suppress a movement in Arizona Territory to make it a Confederate stronghold and calm agitated Indians and Mexicans who wanted their lands back. Banning, the astute businessman, benefited financially from having several thousand troops stationed in his town.

For supplying this number, the US Army experimented with camels to transport materiel overland from Texas. Although mean-spirited and incorrigible, camels were familiar with desert treks and could carry 600-pound loads. This didn't pan out. Soldiers preferred managing mules and horses, and the camels were set loose. One was thought to survive in the wild for another thirty years, and Topsy lived into her 80s at the Los Angeles Zoo.

The buildings of Drum Barracks suffered a slow decimation after the Army decommissioned the fort in 1870. The 19 original structures dwindled to one. It was the junior officers' quarters that survived and was restored as a Civil War Museum, now staffed by volunteers in Civil War (Union) uniforms. Photographs, maps, memorabilia, and a library shelved to the ceiling with relevant books highlight a little-known (at least to me) facet of the Civil War that took place in the Southwest.

Two blocks away, sitting starkly in the middle of an otherwise vacant lot surrounded by chain-link fencing, is the powder magazine where gunpowder for Drum Barracks was stored in wooden kegs. It is a squat brick and stone structure with walls three feet thick. At one point it was rediscovered when a house that entirely surrounded it was demolished. It's worth a walk-by and a moment's reflection on the irony of such a fortified, protective structure once being protected itself by an enveloping structure and now by fencing.

After the war, General Banning expanded his empire by building the first railroad in Southern California, which ran from San Pedro to Los Angeles and cut transit time in half. He was the short-lived owner of this enterprise, however, because more powerful men were extending a rail line from San Francisco to Southern California, and they held Los Angeles hostage by demanding big bucks along with property for their right of way and ownership of Banning's connector line. Otherwise the magnates would bypass LA and leave it unconnected with rail lines that were beginning to crisscross the country. LA and Banning caved.

At the end of the 19th century, Collis Huntington and his empire-building buddies again threatened the commercial viability of San Pedro harbor by promoting their Long Wharf, which extended into Santa Monica Bay 25 miles north, as the designated port for Los Angeles. Ultimately, San Pedro prevailed, and only 10 feet of railroad track memorializing Huntington's dream remain. Contrast that to San Pedro's 113 miles of on dock rails and 82 container cranes prickling the horizon over an expanse of 12 square miles.

I have described San Pedro's and Wilmington's history at some length, and you may be wondering how this backstory contributes to the area's gold-medal status. The answer principally results from the fact that a port of this size has attracted considerable commercial and military attention. Money followed. Consider Phineas Banning, who

bootstrapped himself from a store clerk into a wealthy businessman and built a 30-room mansion in, where else, Wilmington.

Contrasted with adobe haciendas that prevailed in Southern California at the time, the General's Greek Revival home (rectangular, symmetric, large columns, low-pitched gable roof) was a standout. It was built during the Civil War largely by carpenters and blacksmiths from ships berthed in Wilmington Harbor. Banning regally entertained ship captains and encouraged them to stay in port longer to ensure elimination of any leaks, which gave time for their craftsmen to complete Banning's home. For the remaining 20 years of Banning's life, the mansion was a centerpiece for entertaining high rollers in government and commerce.

In 1927 Los Angeles purchased the 20-acre property for a park and restored Victorian-era splendor to the home along with a one-room schoolhouse and the large stable. The Banning family donated many of the original furnishings, which made for an interesting tour of the formal rooms downstairs and the bedrooms upstairs, especially a toy room with fascinating vintage playthings. In the barn, a fully restored "Banning and Co." stagecoach stands ready to transport travelers to LA and beyond.

The second-story front porch of the Banning mansion looks south, toward the harbor, of course. In the near distance, beyond the park's expansive lawn and ornate iron fence, Banning Boulevard extends for four blocks. It, along with the two streets flanking it, is designated a Historic Preservation Overlay Zone.

I talked to a homeowner who was weeding her flower bed. "What does the sign mean?" She half smiled and half frowned. I learned that the HPOZ is an LA city program to protect the character of neighborhoods with distinct architectural and historic character from wanton redevelopment. A neighborhood can vote to become an HPOZ. If the city officials approve the request, residents within the zone must go through an additional review and approval beyond city-wide zoning regulations before performing any exterior work. This would include any addition, new construction, and landscaping visible from the street.

Apparently weeding was not included because she continued with both her explanation and her gardening. Just then a peacock ran across the street. "See that. Those birds tore up my wood shingle roof, and it was agony finding composite shingles that closely matched the original roof in texture and color closely enough to meet the board's approval. However, I do like knowing that an ultramodern box will not be going up next door."

I highly recommend strolling through the neighborhood along Banning Boulevard to appreciate the well-kept, unpretentious homes of considerable architectural variation but without any jarring outliers (other than the nearby and uninhabitable powder magazine). Then enjoy a tour of the Banning estate.

Upon Phineas Banning's death in 1885, his oldest son William took over leadership of the Wilmington Transportation Company. He was asked by the owner of Santa Catalina Island ("twenty-six miles across the sea") to have one of their company's coastal steamers provide regular service between San Pedro and Catalina and thereby promote his vision of turning the island into a tourist destination. William Banning and his younger brothers upped the ante and bought Catalina Island for $129,000 in 1892 (That would be about $4.7 million in 2025—a bargain.) They allowed only their company's boats to land tourists on the island, a monopolistic practice that the courts outlawed in 1907 by declaring Catalina harbor an open port. The brothers sold the island to William Wrigley (chewing gum magnate) and his partners ten years later, and here is how the next story fits into my walk-around.

The principal shipbuilder for both Wrigley and the second generation Bannings was William Muller, an immigrant from Germany. In 1901 he bought a new and yet unoccupied house from the mayor of San Pedro. Because of city construction in 1912, the house was moved on log rollers to a new location two miles south. The docent at the Muller House Museum described that the Muller family slept in the house during the move and used the neighbors' bathrooms along the way.

Muller died in 1936, and the family donated the house to the San Pedro Historical Society. In 1986, it got moved again, a half mile, to its present location, overlooking the harbor as William Muller would have most likely approved.

Muller designed and built many of the wooden passenger ferries, cargo steamers, and yachts that plied the Pacific Coast in the early 1900s. He also made several glass-bottom boats for the Bannings. As a hobby he also built replicas of old-time stagecoaches. To look at the Muller House Museum, it seems far too big to move, but even more remarkable is the woodworking craftsmanship that Muller applied to the fireplace mantels, wall paneling, window molding, on and on. Hardly a surface escaped his tasteful attention.

Most intriguing is a smallish closet where Muller could store five suits and hats. The ensembles were supported on a series of polished hardwood valets tiered front to back and hinged from the

floor such that Muller could lean the front ones forward and access an outfit farther back. He had crafted each valet with a wide opening midway up through which to hang a pair of trousers. Above this was a shoulder-shaped expansion for a jacket. On top was a rounded pedestal for a tie and hat. I am guessing that Muller was a dapper dresser.

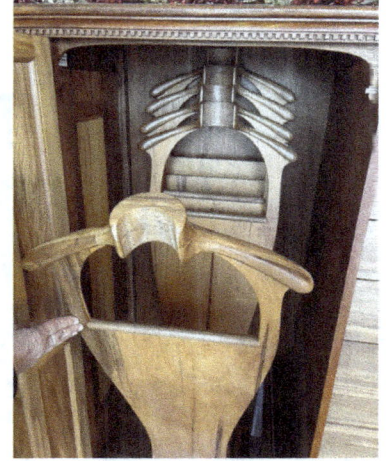

Regardless, for the sake of crafts-manship and local history, the museum is a treasure. When Muller's house was rolling south in 1912, it would have gone by the Vinegar Hill neighborhood, which may have gotten its name from local interest in homebrewing sour wine. Success-ful businessmen in the late 19th and early 20th centuries built modest

single-family homes. A number of them are well preserved and architecturally significant—sufficiently so that the area is another designated Historic Preservation Overlay Zone, like the neighborhood near the Banning mansion. Vinegar Hill styles are said to include Queen Anne, American Four-square, Craftsman, American Colonial, and Spanish Colonial Revival. I can't tell them all apart, but it is pleasant to stroll along the several tree-lined streets to see the many-gabled homes with architectural details that nobody wants to pay for these days.

My favorite is the corner home of a Danish sea captain. It has a second-story wrap-around porch and is topped with a third-story gazebo from which he could survey the harbor.

About the time that home construction on Vinegar Hill began, an ornate Victorian-style lighthouse was built at the southernmost point

of Los Angeles—Point Fermin. The name memorializes a Catholic priest who had been hospitable to the British explorer, George Vancouver. The Point Fermin bluff looks directly across the channel to Catalina Island, which is clearly visible in the distance by day but would have made passage along the coast and into the harbor hazardous in darkness or fog. The light eased navigation under these conditions until 1942, when it was turned off as a security precaution during World War II. After the war, more sophisticated navigational aids made the lighthouse obsolete. Following decades of neglect, it was restored in time for its centennial celebration in 1974 and is now one of San Pedro's most recognized landmarks.

The peaceful park that surrounds the lighthouse includes picnic areas, a concert shell, flower gardens, and several jaw-droppingly beautiful Morton Bay fig trees. The docent on my tour made it clear that however amiable the area is now, a lighthouse keeper in times gone by led a monastic existence, maybe something like that of Father Fermin Francisco de Lasuen.

San Pedro's other lighthouse, not as old or picturesque as the one at Point Fermin, but still functioning, punctuates the end of the two-mile-long breakwater that defines the outer limits of the harbor and protects it from high surf. Angels Gate Lighthouse became fully automated in 1974 and is off limits to visitors, but land lubbers can see it in the distance, and the whale-watching and sport-fishing boats pass nearby on their way in and out of the harbor. Its squatty tower, initially painted completely white, was hard to see in the fog, so vertical black stripes were added, giving it a formal appearance.

What I like best about this lighthouse is that it is slightly tilted. Nobody is sure why. Factors likely include an inadequate foundation, intermittent buffeting by high surf, earthquake shaking, and land subsidence caused by depletion of the Wilmington oil fields. (Some areas of Wilmington subsided by as much as 20 feet before the authorities began pumping salt water underground to replace the support of the extracted oil.) So a striped leaning lighthouse greets every cruise ship and container vessel arriving at LA harbor. My reaction would be, "Wow, this must be a lively place—a mix of order and disorder."

It was, initially, for the Japanese immigrants who established an abalone fishery in the late 19th century at White Point, a cove and beach at the foot of a looming white-faced bluff several miles up the coast from Point Fermin. It was not long after, however, that anti-Japanese sentiment caused the passage of a state law banning the Japanese from this industry. They could, and did, continue to gather and recreate at White Point because of a law that exempted them from operating a sanatorium. On the beach, a hotel, cottages, restaurants, and a large swimming pool, with 82°F water pumped in from nearby sulfur springs, became one of the few places in California where Japanese people could relax, and, if desired, rehabilitate in the mineral baths.

In 1933, a violent earthquake centered in nearby Long Beach damaged the resort's structures and cut off the supply of spring water, so the "sanatorium" was soon abandoned and eventually destroyed by high surf. Well, almost destroyed. A tilted slab from the pool and concrete foundations outlining the footprints of several buildings are still visible among the tide pools on the rocky shore. A vista point on the top of the bluff provides not only a bird's eye view of the remains but also spectacular views up and down the coast and across the channel to Catalina Island. A circular fountain graces the vista point. For decades it lay in ruins among the resort's foundations but was brought to the top of the bluff in 1982 and restored.

If you want another jolt of magnificent scenery clashing with unsettling relics, just turn your back on the fountain and Catalina and look inland. In the near distance is a gently upsloping 102-acre hillside graced with low shrubs, wildflowers, and pathways—the White Point

Nature Preserve. It is great for mountain biking, hiking, dog walking, and bird watching. Along the crest of the hill, a row of houses has commanding views of the seacoast. How serene—that is, until your gaze comes down a bit from the horizon and spots a large eyebrow-shaped concrete structure dug into the slope.

This bomb-hardened bunker sheltered 16-inch guns during WWII that protected the northern approach to the LA harbor. The descriptive plaque says that the steel-reinforced concrete slab is 17 feet thick and that the guns could hurl one-ton projectiles 26 miles. The guns are gone, but the structure looks, well, hard.

Looking down the hill, close to the road are two basketball-court sized areas that are devoid of vegetation. One is surrounded by a low chain-link fence while the other seemingly identical one is not. Both have concrete slabs with several large rusted-metal trap doors and weather-protected air vents with peeling paint. The descriptive plaque is again informative. During the Cold War, Nike surface-to-air missiles lurked underground, ready to protect the coast from Soviet bombers. Neither the guns nor the missiles were ever deployed. Now their associated relics rest quietly in a nature preserve up-bluff from an ocean named for its peaceable quality.

Long before the area became White Point Nature Preserve, it was part of an unnamed military installation intended to improve the defense of the harbor area. In 1914, it was named in honor of General Arthur MacArthur, whose military career spanned 47 years beginning with the Civil War. Fort MacArthur spread over a vast area on three levels of terrain rising from portside and was an active military base until 1975. Then the Army turned the lower and upper levels over to the City of Los Angeles. The lower level was cleared off and dredged to form a pleasure-craft marina. The middle level was transferred to the United States Air Force and later, in 2019, to the United States Space Force, which uses the area for administrative offices and housing. The upper level became Angels Gate Park, which is the location of the model railroad clubs I described, a contemporary art gallery featuring local artists, a youth hostel, playground, picnic area, and a spectacular bird's-eye view of the entire coastal region.

There is a considerable change in elevation in the neighborhood spanning between the middle and upper levels of Fort MacArthur. Twenty-eighth Street connects the two and is titled by some as the steepest street in America, or at least in California, or at least in San Pedro. This ambiguity stems from how aficionados advocate for their favorite. This incline in San Pedro measures 33.3% grade, much greater than even Lombard Street in San Francisco, but it does so for only a 50-foot stretch, which some mountain goats find inadequately long for recognition. Walking it both ways required some concentration and effort, but the experience was entirely eclipsed by what awaited me in the park at Fort MacArthur's upper level.

The park's feature attraction is sited on a grassy knoll at the highest point, the same elevation that initially made the area attractive to military planners. In 1976, the South Korean government gave a bell to the United States to commemorate its bicentennial, to honor Korean War veterans, and to cement the friendship between the two countries. Other sites were considered, but this one resonated with the Korean officials who hold the MacArthur name in great respect. Arthur MacArthur's son, Douglas, was the commander of allied forces that repelled the North Korean invasion and ensured the independence of South Korea. The bronze bell was modeled on one cast in 771 CE, which remains on view in South Korea. The two bells are equally gargantuan—12 feet high and 7.5 feet in diameter—about the size of a small SUV. The bell's average thickness is eight inches, which accounts for its 17-ton weight—five times that of the SUV. These specs rank the two bells among the largest in the world.

Four pairs of figures appear in relief on the Friendship Bell's surface and represent the spirits of freedom, independence, peace, and prosperity in the two countries. The bell has no clapper but is rung by striking it on the outside with a log suspended horizontally on two chains. It is rung on special occasions as well as for a "maintenance ring" on the first Saturday of the month, which serendipitously, was when I happened to visit. Once struck, the deep tone and palpable vibrations reverberate for at least a minute.

The pagoda-like pavilion that houses the bell is equally impressive. Thirty craftsmen from Korea spent almost a year on site building it. A large stone base is flat except for a dished-out area directly under the bell, designed to amplify the sound and direct it upward. Twelve stone columns, representing the signs of the Korean zodiac, support the roof, which is not only stout to suspend the bell, but also graceful and ornate. It exemplifies a centuries-old Korean architectural style. Blue tiles cover the outside, and elegantly carved and painted wood embellish the underside. The park is a world-class spot to take in a sunset or get married.

Returning to the waterfront, more attractions awaited me at my gold-medal Hot Spot. The Saturday Morning Fish Market is more of an attraction for seafood lovers than casual tourists, because it is open to the public only once a week between 2:00 AM and 7:00 AM. At this block-long warehouse of wholesale seafood companies and during these hours, seafood lovers come with their ice chests from all over Southern California to stock up at below retail prices. I arrived at 6:15, and the frenzy was winding down—less shopping, more checking out and loading catches in trunks and truck beds for the trip home. For me, the spectacle was a reminder of edible seafood's variety. Planked out on ice, every fish, whole or filleted, that appears on restaurant menus was represented plus clams, oysters, squid, cuttlefish, and snow crabs. Many varieties were sold out, and only handwritten signs indi-cating type and price remained.

For those interested in ocean life but who are not early risers, the nearby Cabrillo Marine Aquarium displays a far wider variety of critters than seen at the Fish Market, and these are alive and in sea water rather than on ice. There are no dolphin shows, no swimming with the sharks, rather the displayed animals' variety in shape, color, and behavior provides for equally staggering drama on a smaller scale. I particularly liked the sea stars and the moon jellies.

The building itself was designed by noted architect Frank Gehry, but the modest design is eclipsed by the natural beauties that the aquarium contains. Other marine animal attractions in the area include the elusive grunion sex fiends, whose rituals I expose in Chapter 4 (Nature), and the rescued seals and sea lions at the Marine Mammal Care Center, which I describe in Chapter 5 (Nurture).

I hope you can begin to see why an LA-city-limits walker would fall in love with San Pedro and Wilmington—so much to see, densely packed together. Consider that Pinoy Big Mouth restaurant, described in Chapter 12 (Work), is at the extreme north end of Wilmington. Ten miles south is Point Fermin, which is the southern tip of Los Angeles. Along this line at its northern end are the Banning mansion, Drum Barracks, and Channel Street Skate Park (famous because it was a do-it-yourself project that after years of bureaucratic agony became legal). Toward the southern end, the Korean Friendship Bell, the Cabrillo Maritime Aquarium, and the Lane Victory cargo ship museum are clustered. What truly solidifies the area's status as my gold medal winner, however, is a two-mile by half-mile stretch in the middle. I opened this chapter with "nostalgia reigns here." This is its epicenter.

Having just finished the Fish Market, I started at the high side of this rectangle at 7 am on a Saturday morning. Sixth Steet, formerly San Pedro's main shopping street, now a bit sad, slopes gently down to the harbor, lined on both sides by low-rise storefronts. Parked at the curb with the driver's

window down and nobody around was a 1940s black Cadillac coupe about three blocks long and sporting whitewall tires. It was parked in front of the architecturally significant Arcade Building, whose tranquil interior courtyard includes a fountain and a 30-foot-high atrium with a glass skylight extending the entire length of the building. Its Italian Renaissance style stems from an extensive remodel in 1924 of a duplex built by an Italian immigrant.

With its marble floor and oak staircases and wrought iron railings leading to a second-story gallery, it is a gem.

Immediately across the street is the Warner Grand Theater, another gem, which I described in Chapter 13. It stands as another testimony to Sixth Street's glory days. Along the four blocks of Sixth Street to the harbor from the Caddy, Arcade Building, and Warner Grand, several buildings stand empty; the others have been repurposed—vintage record store, hobby shop, Pilates studio, two pizza parlors with seating on the sidewalk, brewery, Subway, Mexican restaurant. You get the picture—similar at first glance to many other town centers whose life has been sucked away by suburban shopping malls and big box stores.

Sixth Street, however, has several other features that uniquely enrich San Pedro. The exposed side wall of the Warner Grand serves as a 4000-square-foot canvas for a commissioned and professionally pro-duced mural, "The Song She Sings." Down the street several blocks, another mural, "Soulful Sunrise Melody," extends over 100 feet along a side walkway. Together they do not hold a candle to Venice in quantity, but the quality equals any I came across in Venice or along Chandler Avenue in North Hollywood.

Halfway to the harbor in a shopping arcade, a front window boldly proclaims The Dog Groomer. Subheadings announce "Medicated Baths," "Aloe Wraps," "Specializing in Senior Dogs," "Therapeutic Skin Treatments," and "Luxurious Mud Treatments." Wow. I checked my GPS. Yep, I was in down-to-earth San Pedro, not Beverly Hills. I went in. They were busy. I was most intrigued by their do-it-yourself pet-wash stations, which were enclosures with large basins, warm water, and blow dryers. I bought a packet of "Mobility Mud" to try on my pooch at home. As I walked on, I understood why all the local dogs were looking so fine.

Embedded in the sidewalk at intervals along this stretch of Sixth Street, triangular bronze plaques memorialize sports heroes. Each plaque simply includes the athlete's name and a symbol for their sport. Initially, most honorees were homegrown; more recently, nationally and internationally recognized greats are included. A larger descriptive plaque concludes, It is hoped that the San Pedro Sportswalk, by memorializing the accomplishments of these sports stars, will be an inspiration for all those who pursue excellence.

Sadly, city-limit walking was not among the sports that are included on the Walk of Fame. I was sufficiently inspired by the heroes' accomplishments, however, to continue to the waterfront. Two blocks to the right stands a US post office building of note. Built in 1935, its exterior only hints of the building's Art Deco/Beaux-Arts/Streamline Moderne styles current in its day and the same as the Coca Cola Building in South LA that I describe in Chapter 13. Inside the post office, interesting details abound, including a marble floor patterned to look like area carpets, public writing desks with

bronze lamps and ink wells, as well as a 40-by-74-foot mural depicting postal workers delivering mail by foot, bike, train, ship, and plane, much more dramatic than the frumpy white putt-putt vehicles that facilitate mail delivery these days.

At the foot of Sixth Street, within a stone's throw of each other along Harbor Boulevard, are three museums, two land based, one floating. I described the Los Angeles Fire Department Harbor Museum (land based) in Chapter 15 (Infrastructure). Across the street is the Los Angeles Maritime Museum. This building, completed in 1941, was originally the Municipal Ferry Terminal building, again designed in the Streamline Moderne style. Exhibits inside include a history of commercial diving in Los Angeles Harbor and a number of models, 10 to 20 feet long, of famous Navy ships, including the cruiser Los Angeles. Upstairs are smaller models of merchant ships from Phoenician times forward. The ships in bottles continue to vex my imagination. Immediately adjacent to the Maritime Museum, whale-watching excursion boats depart.

In a small park en route to the floating museum is the Merchant Marine Memorial, which is reminiscent of the Viet Nam Veterans Memorial in Washington D.C. It features large black polished granite slabs at sidewalk level listing the names of cargo ships destroyed during wartime and the names of their crew members who died. I searched for the names of several of these ships. They were all Liberty ships torpedoed during WWII. Because they were commercial, not military, vessels, they were often managed by sailors too young or insufficiently fit to join the military but who wanted to contribute to the war effort.

Also on display and in keeping with the maritime theme are two fireboats—one mothballed and restored, the other at the ready. A traffic-signal control box has been painted to commemorate the several hundred swimmers from around the world who have completed the 20-mile swim from Catalina to the mainland—a monumental feat considering that those who accomplish it generally begin their journey at midnight to avoid blustering afternoon winds and unpredictable currents. Great white sharks are known to swim in the channel.

Near the control box a gigantic bronze propeller rests on its side. It was removed from the Queen Mary luxury liner as she was being permanently berthed nearby in Long Beach and converted to a museum and hotel. Across a parking lot that is shared with the Los Angeles World Cruise Center and impossible to overlook at dockside is the battleship USS Iowa, now a museum. The length of three football fields and bristling with an array of guns up to 16-inch caliber, it commands respect. Well, at least it did in its time from 1943 to 1990, but it was the last battleship to be built because they became too vulnerable when air attacks became effective. Now restored and staffed mostly by retired Navy veterans, the Iowa shouts of bygone power. The self-guided tour took me from bow to stern, above and below deck. Most surprising were the conning tower midship with its 17-inch-thick steel walls protecting the captain during battle and Vicky's Doghouse on the fantail, serving gourmet hotdogs.

Fine dining in San Pedro and Wilmington is not the norm. Neither is grand opera or haut couture. Rather, eateries reflect the small town, multi-ethnic, working-class heritage of the area. Food options in modest surroundings include Mediterranean, Thai, Italian, Mexican, French, Korean, Japanese, Chinese, Hawaiian, Vietnamese, Filipino, and Lebanese. I finished my hot dog and walked on, preparing to leave my gold-medal treasures and head up the Shoestring toward South LA.

En route, San Pedro surprised me with one more charm—a narrow, tree-lined park almost a mile long, squeezed in between Harbor Boulevard and the water. Officially known as the Harbor Boulevard Parkway Promenade, it includes a bike path, pedestrian walkway, park benches, playground and exercise equipment, and public art. Six-foot-diameter stone medallion inlays that decorate the meandering brick sidewalk invite walkers to pause and reflect on local history. The lengthy inscriptions on each detail the area's railroad connections, the union movement among dock workers, LA's annexation of San Pedro and Wilmington, immigrants contributions, and the importance of the industries of ship building, petroleum extraction, and seafood harvest and canning.

At the north end of the promenade is the Gateway Plaza, with its raised performance platform, and the Fanfare Fountains, which at times create a changing water display. While I sat tranquilly and reflected on all that I had experienced in San Pedro and Wilmington, ducks in the pool seemed to be enjoying the neighborhood as well.

CHAPTER 17

CLOSING THE LOOP

Once I knew its shape and where to look for it, Mt. Lukens was visible for the better part of my entire trek. Climbing it the second time and returning to my starting point was without incident, and the vistas were equally inspiring, except now I could point there, there, and there and see in the distance where I had been—Mission Point, San Pedro, South LA.

When I tell people about my adventure, they often ask, "What attraction did you find most interesting?" That is impossible to say because the points of interest were so varied. Some appealed to my established hobbies, which are as varied as gardening, architecture, and adventure. Others came as complete surprises and enriched my trip in unexpected ways. Among those that I stumbled across were the Platinum Prop House, Sims House of Poetry, and warehouses stuffed with spices, buttons, candy, Christmas decorations, or caskets. These proprietors, along with museum docents and those caring for disadvantaged children, bees, rescued guinea pigs, and injured marine mammals genuinely love what they do. Their level of commitment is inspiring and infectious.

I agree with country and western singer Luke Bryan, who sings, "Most people are good." This was reaffirmed many times. For example: a FedEx driver and several homeowners offered me water; a handyman asked if I wanted a ride when he confirmed that my next destination was several miles ahead; and I heard passengers departing the bus say, "Thank you" to the driver. Bryan continues by singing, "I believe, if you just go by the nightly news, your faith in all mankind would be the first thing you lose."

Other surprises? One thought that attracted me to the idea of circumambulating LA was the convoluted shape of its city limits. It haunted me to the point that I have seen several accidental oil or paint smears on the pavement that struck me as having the same shape as LA's border. "Rorschach test? Is this a message?" Thinking others would be equally fascinated by LA's outline, I featured it prominently on business cards I passed out and printed it on the T-shirts I regularly wore. But other than the rare person recognizing "The Shoestring," nobody expressed interest in the manic zigzags. I guess most people don't like maps as much as I do. Everyone seemed fascinated by the idea of my adventure. Upon learning of it, the most frequent responses were, "That is so cool," "No way," and "Awesome."

I was also surprised that despite walking an average of ten miles a day twice a week, I did not lose any weight. And my walking shoes, which I replaced with boots on the wilderness segments, did not show any appreciable wear. Again and again, I was tricked by my two-dimensional maps, which do not indicate changes in elevation. But I would forget that and have to huff and puff up three-mile-long inclines and sweat and swear during the descent from Castle Peak.

My saddest surprise was being made aware of LA's history of racism. I lived my first 28 years sequentially in Kansas City, Houston, Nashville, and Baltimore—fringes of the South, so I was aware of the past and sometimes presence of interracial issues. When I moved to California decades ago, those issues seemed to be far behind. The trek changed that. Yet, I still believe that most people are good.

Danger? On the entire trip, I encountered only one clearly risky situation—the steep, gravelly slope creating a treacherous and nearly impossible scramble and skid down from Castle Peak. Carl and I were in over our heads that day, which we discovered only after it was too late to turn back. We were lucky we did not break anything or lose something dearer than one cell phone. By comparison, riding the region's buses, walking along a few narrow busy roads, and traversing some neighborhoods, which have in the past been considered "sketchy" if not outright dangerous, were not problematic.

In that regard, here was my worst encounter. Walking along a major street, which was my modus operandi, a neatly dressed fellow coming toward me asked for a dollar. As is my habit, I said no. He looked at my trekking poles and asked where I was going and then helped me with directions. He also pointed out that I had a streak of sunblock on my face and ensured that I rubbed it away. I gave him two dollars.

Injuries? I sustained two. The first was a slow fall on the first day onto the uphill side of the trail on Mt. Lukens. This resulted in a mildly skinned knee and elbow and a broken trekking pole. The other was a blister sustained well into the trip one day when I unwisely wore thin socks.

Disappointments? By far the biggest letdown was being stood up three times by the grunions.

Other downers related to phantom attractions. On the enlarged Google map, I found pins indicating curiosities such as locations for having a caricature drawn, an outdoor wedding performed, and a guard dog hired. Alas, when I walked by these addresses, they were just private residences without artists, justices of the peace, or canines in evidence.

Considering my criterion that attractions had to be within a mile inside the city limits line, other potential points of interest were, to my disappointment, out of range. If I had loosened this requirement, I could have thrown axes, vented my hostility in a rage room, and checked in on a business called MeUndies.

I could also have visited Mission San Fernando and a nearby historic stone building used for public meetings. It honors a back-to-the-land activist named Bolton Hall. I think this gathering spot should be called Bolton Hall Hall, but somehow the details got lost, and now it is just Bolton Hall.

More attractions in Griffith Park would have also been in range, including Bronson Cave, the Hollywood sign, the Greek Theatre, and the Observatory. I finally forgave the grunions because they did reveal themselves on my fourth try.

Relief? A gentlemen's club (strip club) was closed when I happened by midmorning. I had mixed feelings about returning when it was open. Sure, I wanted to be thorough and experience a broad range of activities without being selective or judgmental, so I researched it and found that it was one of a chain of clubs. Therefore without guilt or shame, I skipped it for the same reason that I bypassed Targets, Taco Bells, and other multi-location enterprises.

Regrets? In the early days of the trip I occasionally found myself too focused on completing that day's mileage goal rather than savoring surprises I encountered along the way. On different days I walked past two "characters" who likely had interesting stories, but being on the move, I didn't stop to talk to them. One was a young man perched on the top of the bench at a bus stop with spiked hair, reflective sunglasses, eclectic garb, and caressing a skateboard. The other was a man of indeterminate age whom I passed on a weekday morning in a residential neighborhood—top hat, red bow tie, and, I think, tails. After that, I slowed down and sometimes backtracked to take it all in. I still try to do the same.

Joy? I loved seeing the Labrador retriever pups cavort at Guide Dogs of America | Tender Loving Canines and learning how, with training, they would make monumental changes in the lives of their adopted owners, who were vision impaired or experiencing PTSD.

Plans? I was about a fourth of the way along my trek and walking through a residential neighborhood in the Woodland Hills area of the San Fernando Valley. Curbside, a gardener in his twenties was transferring recently raked leaves into a large green barrel. We chatted about gardening. He was surprised to hear that I did my own. I asked him how many clients he had up and down the street. He said he had a full complement of clients scattered over a ten-mile radius. He was thereby establishing his reputation in a wide area so he could eventually hire associates and develop a full-service landscape company. He had a plan.

I told him about my trek, including that I still had about 240 miles and several months to go. Forward thinker that he clearly was, he asked, "What are you going to do next?" I confessed that I did not have a plan. As I continued my walk, his straightforward question stuck with me. I thought, "What is next? Stay home and get old? No. Walk the other direction? Outside rather than inside the line?"

Toward the end of my trek I took a break and went hiking for a week in the Swiss Alps with a buddy. We stayed at a mountain hotel near the end of a tortuous one-lane road halfway up a glaciated valley. The municipal minibus pulling a covered trailer came by every two hours and deposited day hikers outside our hotel's breakfast room.

One hiker stood out among the senior ladies' groups and the couples ranging in age from young adulthood to past retirement age. He was slender and topped with snow-white hair. His beard, equally white, would immediately qualify him for seasonal work as Santa Claus. Trekking poles in hand, off he went.

Later that day my buddy and I met him on the trail. He was hiking by himself and moving steadily up a route that the AllTrails app appropriately classified as moderate. Communication was limited because of the disparities between his Swiss German and Steve's and my unpolished Hoch Deutsch. What came through clearly, however, was "achtundachtzig." This hiker was 88 years old—and still hiking. How inspiring!

So when I am his age, I want to be doing what he was enjoying that day—staying active, discovering, learning outside his neighborhood.

How about you? What's next?

photo by Thomas Bumbera

ACKNOWLEDGMENTS

Walking solo on my trek facilitated introspection. It also catalyzed interesting conversations with people I randomly encountered. On some days, however, I enjoyed having walking companions— namely, Tammie Bardowell, Michael Esser, Thomas Bumbera, Carl Singerman, and Kathy and Prosper Benhaim. They enriched my experience by pointing out details I would have overlooked— adding perspective and insights; and, for certain segments, providing comfort in numbers.

My wife, Susan, accompanied me on several "infill" visits that involved returning to attractions that were closed when I first walked by. As with my walking companions, Susan enlightened me with her observations, expanding my experience and giving context to our many conversations about my walk. For more than fifty years, Susan has supported my adventuresome tendencies and monastic writing habits with love and gentle guidance.

Some points of interest practically demanded companionship in order to have meaning. My longtime friends Amy and Phil Jackson enthusiastically accepted my invitations for weird activities such as savoring Filipino street food and watching the silvery grunions flop about late at night. Phil and I competed in go-kart racing. And, along with Alex Jamai, my trainer, we cooperated to escape from a phony cannibalistic killer. Alex also ensured that I exhibited good form while pumping iron in the Pen at Muscle Beach.

Charles Rosenberg, Vern Tolo, and Lyne Robe read early versions of the manuscript and offered valuable suggestions for improvement. Thanks also go to Carrie Cantor for line editing the manuscript. With great skill, she improved the style and structure of my writing to ensure that it conveyed my intended meaning. Renee Pulve's graphic design talents are equally monumental and appreciated. She produced the graphics for the T-shirt I wore every trekking day and the business cards I gave to those expressing interest in my adventure. She also designed the book's eye-catching cover. When it was first published, I was satisfied that the book was free of typos. How wrong I was. Thank you, Marla Wilson, for painstakngly documenting these during an early read and gently educating me on some fine and overlooked points of grammar, now fixed.

I took over 2400 photos along the way. One hundred are included in the book. Thank you, iPhone 14.

A final note of gratitude goes to all the Angelenos I encountered on my trek. They are an inspiring assortment of people who took time to share their passions with me. I encourage you to get out there, take a walk outside your neighborhood, and meet folks like them.

******

To help potential readers know whether *Walking the Line* is right for them, please rate the book on Amazon by scanning the QR code. A brief review, indicating what you liked and didn't like about the book would also be helpful. Thanks.

INDEX

Please let other readers know if *Walking the Line* would be right for them. Amazon and Goodreads ratings and reviews will help.

Follow all of Dr. Meals' bookish explorations.
AboutMuscleAnd Bone.info
X @lacitylimits
Facebook @lacitylimits
Instagram @lacitylimits_

Possible Book Club Discussion Points

What were your initial expectations for *Walking the Line*? Did the book exceed, meet, or disappoint your expectations?

Which chapter did you like the best? Least? Why?

Would black and white photos have been sufficient? Would you have liked to have seen more photos?

Did the book change the way you think about LA's boundaries, neighborhoods, or identity? Did it change the way you think about other cities?

What was the author's narrative voice? Did it positively or negatively influence your interest?

Were there instances when the author's personal observations especially enriched or diminished the story?

Did the book enhance your understanding of LA's cultural diversity via its foods, neighborhoods, and local color? If so, how? If not, why?

Which discovery or activity did you find most interesting? Were any boring or too detailed?

The chapters are thematically arranged. Would you have preferred a sequential, day-by-day "diary?"

Does the book inspire readers to explore their own environs in new ways? Will they actually do it? Why or why not?

What is one question that you would like to ask the author?